The World of Cats

A Fully Illustrated Guide to the Fascinating Feline

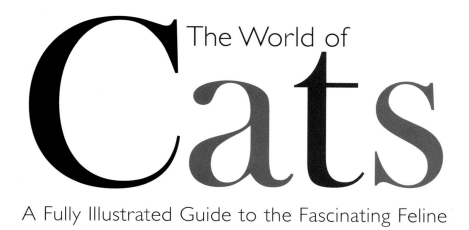

The World of Cats

A Fully Illustrated Guide to the Fascinating Feline

Marianne Mays

GRAMERCY BOOKS
NEW YORK

Acknowledgements

The publisher gratefully acknowledges the help of the following in supplying
photography for this book:
Chanan Photography:
pages 2, 38, 39, 40, 43, 45, 50, 55, 71, 97, 100, 102, 113, 114, 115 (both), 117, 123, 124;
Paddy Cutts/Animals Unlimited:
front cover, pages 7, 15, 27, 29, 33, 34, 35, 36, 37 (both), 41, 42, 46, 47 (top), 48, 49, 51, 53,
54, 57, 58, 59 (both), 60, 61, 62, 63, 64, 65, 66, 70, 72, 73, 75, 79, 81, 83 (bottom), 86, 89,
91, 92, 93, 94, 95 (top), 96, 101, 103, 108, 109, 107, 111 (both), 112, 127;
Animal Photography (Sally Anne Thompson):
back cover, pages 9, 10, 11, 12, 14, 17, 19, 20, 21, 22, 23 (all), 25, 74, 87 (both),
95 (bottom), 105;
Animal Photography (R T Willbie):
page 31;
Alan Robinson/RSPCA Photolibrary:
pages 47 (bottom), 52, 76, 77, 82, 83 (top), 85, 88, 98, 99, 110, 116, 121, 122, 125;
Opurrtune – George and Tracy Oraas:
pages 67, 68;
Larry Johnson Photography:
pages 69, 80, 84, 106, 118, 119, 120.

This 1999 edition is published by Gramercy Books™,
a division of Random House Value Publishing, Inc.,
201 East 50th Street, New York, New York, 10022.
by arrangement with PRC Publishing Ltd, London.

Gramercy Books™ and design are registered trademarks of
Random House Value Publishing, Inc.
Random House
New York • Toronto • London • Sydney • Auckland
http://www.randomhouse.com/

Printed and bound in China
A CIP catalogue record for this book is available from the Library of Congress.

ISBN 0-517-16127-3

8 7 6 5 4 3 2 1

Contents

Introduction

Whether it's a pampered purebred or a run-of-the-mill mixed breed, more and more cats can be found as household pets, bringing their grace and charm to families the world over.

This beautiful Cream Colorpoint Persian will need regular grooming throughout its life to keep it looking so attractive.

And why not? They are fastidiously clean, easy to keep, inexpensive, and beautiful. They make excellent hot water bottles, sinuous table ornaments, and the purr of a stroked cat will reduce the blood pressure of even the most stressed urbanite.

The cats shown on the following pages are not ordinary: bred for color, coat, and breed standards, these are the top cats of the feline world and show well the diversity of this complex, highly evolved species.

Evolution

How much you need to groom your cat depends largely on its coat type. Shorthaired cats will need very little grooming, as they tend to keep their coats in good condition themselves. But they will still need a helping hand to help prevent fur balls.

More than thirty million years ago *Proailurus* — the prehistoric ancestor of today's cat — hunted for prey in the jungles and forests which covered most of the land. Immediately recognizable as the forerunner of the cats to be found in this book, *Proailurus* would evolve into *Pseudailurus*, which would itself evolve into eight groups of animals, one of which includes today's domestic cat.

It was some time before man domesticated the cat — the ancient Egyptians are said to have been the first around 2000BC. The Egyptians used cats as hunters of rodents in grain stores — a function for which farmers would continue to use them until industrialization. The Egyptians worshipped animals as zooamorphic representations of the gods. The feline sun-goddess Bastet, for example, originally represented as a woman with the head of a lioness — a manifestation of the anger of the sun-god Re' — was softened in the Ptolemaic period to become the goddess of pleasure and is often pictured with a cat's head. Cats in her temple were mummified at their death.

Effective rodent killers, cats played a great part in Egyptian life, so much so that one ancient Persian king, aware of the high esteem in which the Egyptians held cats, made each of his soldiers carry a cat into battle, knowing the warring Egyptians would rather give up their fight than risk harming a feline. The Romans, in their turn, venerated the cat — the Roman goddess of Liberty was depicted with a cat lying at her feet — as did many other cultures.

Had the Europeans of the fourteenth century continued this tradition it is possible that the predations of the bubonic plague might not have been so fierce. But so many cats had been killed, many as witches' familiars (it was said that witches took on the shape of cats to go about their evil nighttime business), that when the bubonic plague arrived in Europe in the fourteenth century, it killed millions of people. Soon the cat's low status was reversed and they were again recognized for the valuable contribution they made to human society.

Cats have always been valuable in agricultural economies and they transferred their skills to factories and warehouses during the industrial revolution. Cats are are also closely associated with seafaring and even up to the middle of the twentieth century, cats were important on ships as the only practical way of keeping down the rodent population.

Modern poisons and agricultural methods may have reduced this importance, but the ties between humans and felines have been shown to be stronger than simply as workmates. In the last fifty years cats have taken on the role of family pets and today, particularly in urban surroundings, they are more numerous than dogs. As pets, however, they have lost none of *Proailurus*'s hunting instincts, as is shown by any study of small rodent and bird populations.

Cat Care

Before acquiring a pet cat, regardless of the breed, every prospective owner should be aware of the responsibilities that owning a cat entails. The cat is known for its independent nature, but in no way does this mean that a cat can be left to fend for itself; all cats need at least feeding, grooming, and veterinary treatment. Exactly how a cat needs to be cared for depends to a large extent on its age, and also breed and/or coat type. Kittens, for instance, will need feeding more frequently than adult cats, and longhaired cats will need more extensive grooming than shorthaired cats.

Feeding

Right: Cats usually make excellent mothers and have very little difficulty in caring for their kittens. It is advisable to keep visitors away for the first few weeks though, as the mother may feel threatened and hide her young.

Below: All good pet stores will sell many brands of special kitten food that will provide the essential nutrients to allow it to develop well.

Kittens

Ideally, all kittens would stay with their mothers until the age of twelve weeks. At this age the kitten will be fully weaned, independent of its mother, and also old enough to have been fully inoculated. Sadly, many kittens, in particular non-pedigree kittens, are sold at a much too early age, sometimes as early as six weeks of age. If acquiring such a young kitten, the buyer needs to be aware of the extra responsibilities that this entails.

Kittens up to the age of twelve weeks will need five meals a day. This is in addition to the mother cat's milk, if they are still kept with her. If there is no mother cat (known as a queen) present, a milk supplement needs to be given for the kitten to be able to thrive. Pet stores and veterinary surgeries sell excellent milk replacement formulas specifically manufactured for cats. Kittens should be fed on highly concentrated food rich in protein; special kitten foods is available in many different brands, of either the complete dry or canned type. It is important to realize that a kitten must not be fed on food intended for adult cats, as this will not enable them to develop naturally. A kitten has a very small stomach, yet needs twice as many nutrients as an adult cat, so for a kitten to receive as much as it needs of all the vital nutrients, the food has to be concentrated. Kitten food is manufactured to be very concentrated, and to contain all a growing kitten's requirements. Food for adult cats is much less concentrated, and a kitten surviving on this may after a period of time fall ill with diarrhea, weight loss, and stunted growth.

From the age of twelve weeks, four meals a day will be sufficient, and no milk meal is necessary. From sixteen weeks onward, three meals should be adequate, and by the age of nine months, when the kitten officially becomes an adult cat, two meals a day is all that is needed, and by now the food can also be switched to a diet for adult cats.

Kittens, like any babies, need a lot of sleep. Any children in the household should be made aware of the fact that when the kitten goes to sleep, it must be left alone to rest. Once awake, the kitten will be very active and playful, and all kittens enjoy nothing more than playing games with various toys—preferably toys intended for kittens, with no small parts that may become detached and accidentally swallowed.

Adult cats

A cat is considered adult once it has reached the age of nine months. An adult cat will need two meals a day, with no snacks in between, to avoid becoming overweight. There are many different types and brands of cat food available from pet stores, supermarkets, and also veterinary surgeries. It can be quite bewildering to choose the correct food; if unsure, ask a vet for advice, or the breeder of your cat if it is a pedigree.

Cats need a large amount of protein to be able to stay healthy and, unlike dogs, cannot survive on a vegetarian diet. Most cat foods are excellent, and once you have found a food that seems to suit your cat, stick to this and do not change the diet. Cats can be very picky eaters, and many will start to refuse their food if they believe something even better may be forthcoming. By feeding your cat the same food each day (varying between the different flavors available of most foods is fine) you will make sure that your cat will not suffer from any digestive upsets that a sudden change of diet may cause.

Adult cats should not be given milk to drink, just water, which must be available at all times—in particular if the cat is fed on a complete dry diet. Milk is unnecessary for adult cats, and many cats have delicate stomachs which cannot tolerate milk. Milk is also more a type of food than just a drink, and so a cat prone to putting on weight may well become overweight if given milk to drink.

Old cats

Many cats live for a very long time, into their teens or even longer, but generally speaking, a cat can be considered to be a "senior citizen" from about the age of eight years onward. Older cats will be less active than young cats, and so usually need less food and less protein than young cats. Many cat food manufacturers now make diets specifically for senior cats, and it's a good idea to switch to this type of food once your cat has reached the age of eight.

Kidney problems are common in older cats, with chronic kidney disease often seen in cats aged six and over. For such cats, a special veterinary diet will be required. If fed on such a kidney-friendly diet, your cat should be able to live life to its full for several years, despite dysfunctioning kidneys. Kidney-friendly diets are available in either dry or canned form, and are normally only sold through veterinary surgeries, on prescription from the vet who has diagnosed the cat's condition.

Adult cats will need two meals a day to stay in healthy condition. Nibbling a little grass helps to combat furballs by acting as an emetic.

House Training

Unlike dogs, cats do not normally require formal house training. Kittens will learn by example; they will watch their mother use a litter tray, and will start to copy her from the age of four or five weeks. Even cats that have not been used to living indoors seem to readily accept a litter tray and understand what its purpose is. All that is necessary when acquiring a new cat or kitten is to show it where the litter tray is kept, and the rest should follow naturally.

There are many different types of both litter tray and cat litter available these days. Which types cats prefer can be very individual. Most cats seem to prefer the hooded litter trays, where they can get some privacy, and this is also a popular type with owners as it to a certain extent disguises any unpleasant smells. Which litter to choose is an individual choice; there are clay-based litters, wood-based litter, corn-based litters, and paper-based litters. Absorbency varies from brand to brand, as do how well they reduce the smell. Choose a litter that you like the look of, and see how your cat likes it. If needs be, try a different brand next time.

It is very important to keep the litter tray as clean as possible. Ideally, any soiled litter should be removed daily. Many cats will refuse to use a dirty litter tray, and may instead find alternative spots to use as a toilet area. If two or more cats are kept, it is a good idea to keep several litter trays at various locations in the home.

Never place the litter tray close to where you feed your cat, as no animal likes to eat close to its toilet area!

Right: Unlike dogs, cats do not normally require any formal house training. Kittens will learn by example.

Below: Cats are naturally very clean animals and will sometimes refuse to use a litter tray if it is dirty.

Vaccinations

This Siamese cat is receiving a vaccination from the vet. Although the injection is very quick and relatively painless, the cat may feel nervous. Holding it so that it cannot see the syringe and speaking to it in a reassuring voice should help to calm the cat during the procedure.

All cats need to be inoculated regularly against the major fatal feline diseases, and this is regardless of whether the cat is allowed outdoors or not. Viral infections can be brought into a home simply by the means of the owner walking through an infected area, so no cat is fully protected from disease unless vaccinated. Boarding catteries will always require proof of vaccination before they accept to care for any cat, and in the UK cat shows cannot be entered unless a vaccination certificate signed by a vet can be provided. In the US, it is common for cat breeders to vaccinate their cats personally; in the UK this is not possible. It is always a good idea to have a vet vaccinate your cat, as not only will the cat then be protected against the major diseases, it will also receive a full general health check-up.

All cats needs to be vaccinated against feline enteritis (FIE) and feline influenza ("cat flu"). Both are fatal diseases which can seldom be cured if contracted. It is also possible to vaccinate against feline leukemia virus (FeLV), a fatal disease spread between cats via saliva. FeLV is unlikely to be contracted by an indoor cat which has no contact with outdoor roaming cats. The other fatal disease is feline immunodeficiency virus (FIV), for which there is as yet no vaccine available. Feline chlamydia is a respiratory and ocular disease which is sometimes vaccinated against, although this is not a fatal disease. Rabies vaccinations will be required in certain parts of the US, and certainly for any US-based cat that has access to the outdoors. Always discuss your cat's vaccination program with your vet, as he or she will be the best placed person to advise.

Normally, kittens are first vaccinated against FIE and cat flu at the age of nine weeks, with a second injection given at twelve weeks. Ideally, any kitten sold should have received these two injections. Yearly booster injections are then needed to keep up the cat's immunity to the diseases.

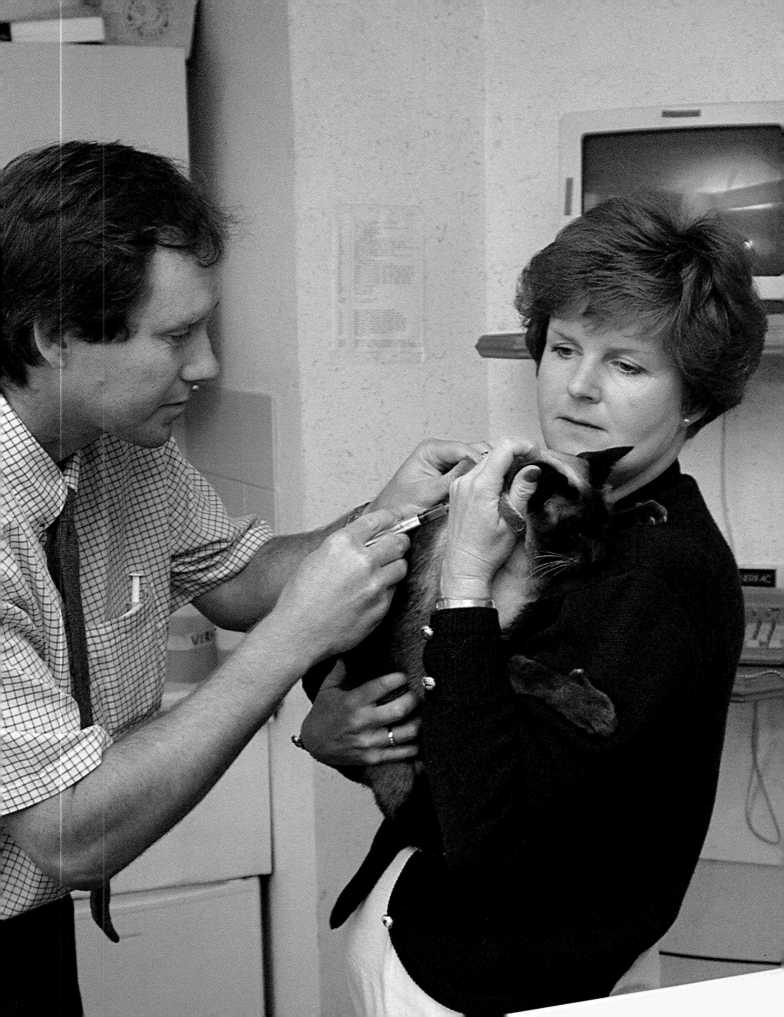

Neutering

Many pedigree breeders these days have their kittens neutered before allowing them to go to their new homes.

Any pet cat not required for breeding should be neutered. Non-pedigree cats should be neutered as routine, as there are already far too many unwanted non-pedigree cats in the world, in desperate need of good homes. By allowing your non-pedigree cat to have kittens you are adding to this problem, and so the only responsible action is to have your pet neutered. Many cat owners believe that a female cat should be allowed to give birth to a litter of kittens before she is neutered, as it will be good for her, but this is nothing but an old wives' tale. A cat that has never had kittens will never miss the experience. In fact, a queen that has given birth may well miss the experience as she will know the joys of motherhood, and so it is much kinder to have her neutered without letting her have kittens first.

There are no health benefits whatsoever in allowing the queen one litter before neutering. Some non-pedigree owners argue that they love their pet dearly and so much would like a litter of kittens from her to enable them to keep a kitten, and that they already have friends and family lined up, all willing to give a home to one kitten each. This may well be the case, but when considering that thousands of cats have to be put to sleep every year simply due to being unwanted, anyone should be able to see that it will make more more sense to give a home to a homeless cat or kitten instead.

The same is, of course, true of pedigree cats. The simple fact that a cat has a pedigree and is purebred does not necessarily make it suitable for breeding. Only the best cats should be used for further breeding; those that closely conform to the breed standards as regards looks and temperament. Just as it is difficult to find enough good homes for non-pedigree kittens, pedigree breeders often find it hard to find suitable homes for any kittens that do not make the grade as show cats.

Breeding cats is an expensive hobby, and the costs involved will be virtually the same regardless of whether you plan to rear a non-pedigree or pedigree litter, if it is to be carried out in a responsible way. Before mating, both the male and the female cat will need to be blood tested to ensure that neither carry any fatal diseases such as feline leukemia virus (FeLV) or feline immunodeficiency virus (FIV)—both incurable and fatal, and both spread via cat-to-cat contact, in particular mating. The pregnant queen will need extra care and more food than usual during her pregnancy, and the actual birth may incur veterinary costs if any complications should arise. To rear the kittens will mean extra outlay for kitten food, large extra amounts of cat litter, and then all kittens will need to be vaccinated before going to their new homes no earlier than at the age of twelve weeks. Pedigree kittens should also be registered with the relevant cat registry. All in all an expensive process, and not something for the novice to enter into lightly.

Needless to say, it is just as important to neuter male cats. Any male cat that is allowed outdoors will mate with female cats, and as such will give rise to unwanted kittens. He will also be at great risk from contracting FeLV or FIV, and will get into serious fights with other entire males. Unneutered male cats are prone to urine marking both indoors and outdoors, and their urine has a very unpleasant strong smell. Likewise, an entire queen will often urinate in inappropriate places when in season (known as "calling"), and unless mated, she may come into call every three weeks all year round if kept in a centrally heated house. When she is in call, she will scream loudly for a mate, will not eat, and if her calls are allowed to go on indefinitely, she may develop medical problems such as fallopian cysts.

In the US, many pedigree breeders these days have their kittens neutered before allowing them to go to their new homes. In the UK, most cats are neutered at the age of six months. Consult your vet for advice on when to neuter your cat. It is a routine operation which will cause the cat little or no discomfort, is cheap to have carried out, and will make your pet a homeloving, friendly companion. It is true that neutered cats easily put on weight, but as long as the cat is fed on a good diet and not overfed, this need never be a problem.

Indoor or Outdoor Cat?

Right: If the cat is allowed to roam outside it will be quite adventurous so it is very important that it is vaccinated against any diseases that it might contract during its travels. The outside world is also full of fleas and other parasites so the coat should be checked for these regularly during grooming.

Below: It is unusual for a pedigree kitten like this Persian to be an outdoor cat.

Whether to allow your cat free outdoor access or not is a big decision. In the US, many cat shelters/rescue societies will not rehome cats to people that will allow them to go outside. In the UK, the reverse is true. Most pedigree cat breeders will much prefer it if their kittens are going to be indoor pets.

Many people believe that a cat cannot be happy unless it is free to roam out of doors. This is simply not true. A cat that has lived indoors all its life will never miss the experience of going out. This is particularly true of pedigree cats, which have been bred indoors for generations. The urge to go out and hunt is simply not there. Many non-pedigree cats do like to go outside, but there are many factors to consider before making the decision.

First of all, where do you live? If it is anywhere near a heavily trafficked road, then it is not a good idea to let a cat out. If you live in a highrise apartment block, again letting the cat out will be impossible. Cats can live very happily in apartments, as long as they are given plenty of stimulation indoors in the form of toys, scratching posts, etc.

Secondly, consider the risks. Any cat that goes outside is running the risk of getting hit by a car, even on small roads, being attacked by dogs or wild animals, and when meeting other cats (in particular strays) the risk of becoming infected with incurable fatal diseases such as feline leukemia virus and feline immunodeficiency virus will always be there. As mentioned earlier, it is possible to vaccinate against FeLV, but not against FIV (see page 16). Studies often show that cats that are allowed outdoors have a markedly shorter lifespan than cats that are kept indoors only.

If you live in a house with a garden, you may want to consider fencing and netting all or part of it, or buying an enclosed run for your cat. That way he or she will be able to spend time outside, but in the safety of your own back yard.

One or Two Cats?

Whether to acquire two kittens or just one is a personal choice, but generally speaking two kittens will not be so much twice the work as twice the fun. Cats greatly love companionship and will very much appreciate a friend of the feline kind, especially if their owner goes out to work during the day. Which sex to choose is less important as both males and females make equally good pets—provided, of course, that they are neutered.

Grooming

Right and inset: Shorthaired cats such as this Siamese will need little grooming. Nevertheless, some attention with a soft brush will remove dead hair and keep the coat looking shiny and attractive. Running a soft cloth over the cat's fur will also add an extra sheen.

Below: Cats need regular grooming throughout their lives so it is important that they become accustomed to it from an early age. The grooming ritual should be a pleasurable experience for the cat as well as a time for owner and cat to bond.

How much you need to groom your cat depends largely on its coat type. Shorthaired cats will need very little grooming, as they tend to keep their coats in good condition themselves. As long as a good diet is fed, the cat's coat should stay nice and shiny. All the same, a weekly grooming session with a slicker brush or fine-toothed metal comb will help to remove any old, dead hairs, especially when the cat is shedding fur. Rex-coated cats need no grooming at all—their coats are so short that they virtually cannot be combed! However, it is a good idea to brush the coat now and then. The hairless Sphynx will need the occasional bath to clean excess grease and dirt from the naked skin.

Semi-longhair cats will need a twice-weekly combing and brushing. Use a metal comb, either one with fine teeth or one with teeth of varying lengths (known as a moulting comb) and pay particular attention to the fur behind the ears, in the armpits, on the stomach, chest, and the "trousers" on the hind legs, as this is where knots and mats will form. Finish off the grooming session by using a soft-bristled brush.

Longhaired cats, i.e. Persians, need extensive grooming. Most Persians need a thorough grooming session three times a week, some may need it daily, depending on how full their coat is. For a Persian, at least two different combs will be needed: a wide-toothed metal comb and a fine-toothed metal comb. A moulting comb is also very useful, as is a slicker brush. The entire coat should first be combed through using the wide-toothed comb, and once that moves freely through the fur, switch to the finer comb. Finish off by brushing with the slicker brush. Remember to pay particular attention to the problem areas—the same as for semi-longhaired cats. A gentle sprinkling of talcum powder (unperfumed) will help to keep the Persian coat grease-free and easy to groom. Persians will also need bathing occasionally, when the coat starts to look greasy.

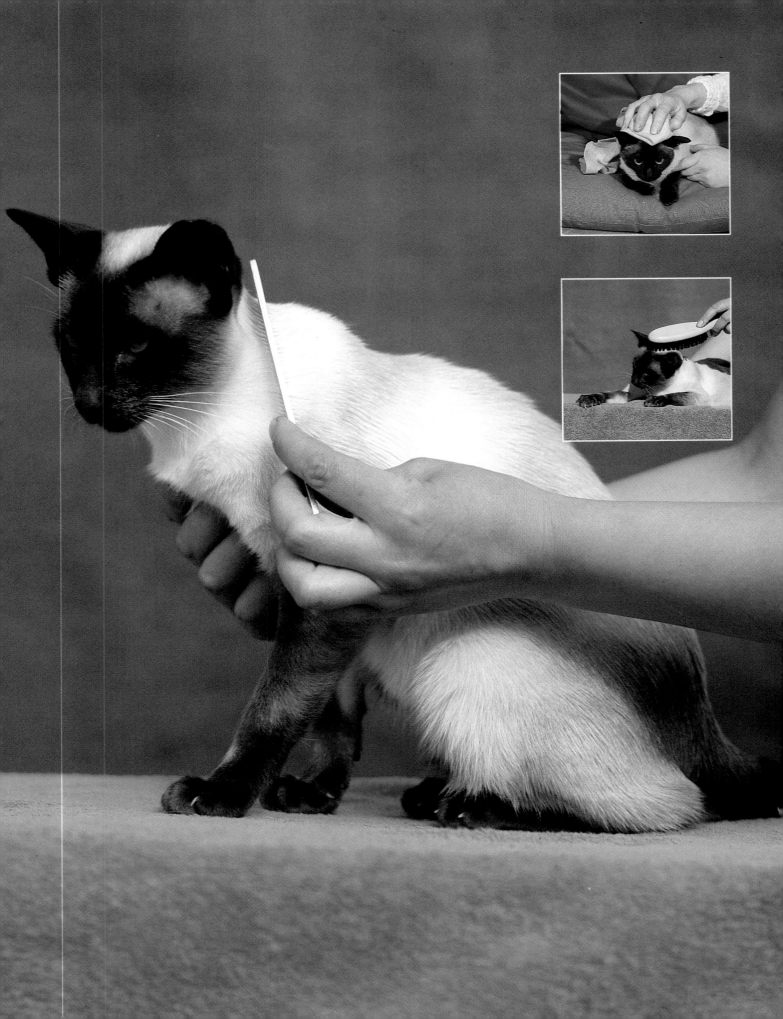

Equipment

Cats do not generally need a lot of expensive equipment, but there are still items that will be essential.

- A litter tray for any indoor cat.
- Food and water bowls.
- A secure cat carrier, for transporting the cat to and from the vet, boarding cattery, cat shows, etc.
- Brush and/or comb, depending on the coat type of your cat.
- A scratching post or so-called cat tree, for your cat to exercise its claws on if indoors—if this is introduced to the cat at an early age it will greatly save your furniture from being damaged!
- Toys will be appreciated by all indoor cats; pet stores stock a large variety of these.

Approaches to Cat Care

In the US, most cat owners, particularly of pedigree cats, realize that allowing a cat outdoors is fraught with risks, and keep their cats indoors. Many shelters also make this a requirement for adoption. In the UK, the major cat rescue organizations have the opposite view, and will only rehome cats to people with a garden, living in an area not too close to major roads.

Neutering in the US is often carried out when the kitten is as young as ten or twelve weeks, to ensure that the cat's new owner does not breed from it. In the UK, the common age for neutering is around six months of age.

Vaccinations and general healthcare differ as well. In the US cat breeders can purchase vaccines and antibiotics and treat their cats themselves; in the UK this has to be carried out by a veterinary surgeon. There is also a greater variety of vaccines available in the US; there is a vaccine against the fungal skin disease ringworm, for instance, which is not available in the UK.

In the US, cats are frequently declawed. This operation involves cutting off the claw and the first toe joint, and is done to stop the cat from scratching items such as furniture. A kinder option is also used, that of sheathing each claw in plastic, thus rendering the claw useless. In the UK, these practices are seen as unacceptable, and vets do not carry out such operations. Declawed cats cannot be shown either—which is also the case with many of the US registries.

Other than this, both the US and the UK share the fact that the cat is the most popular pet, and the number of cat owners are constantly growing.

A cat will need to be transported on a regular basis, particularly if taking part in shows. A good carrier will be comfortable, secure, and allow the cat to see something of its surroundings.

Breed Classification

Just as there are variations in how cats are treated as pets, there are large differences between the pedigree cat scene in the US and in the UK.

In the US, the different breeds of pedigree cats are very broadly classified as either Shorthair or Longhair breeds. To confuse matters, within some registries a breed that was originally accepted as a Shorthair breed, such as the Scottish Fold, may then have a longhaired version added— but still remain in the Shorthair breed group.

In the UK, the breeds are divided into seven different groups: Longhair, Semi-longhair, British Shorthair, Burmese, Foreign, Oriental, and Siamese. Breeds are grouped not according to their origin but purely on their looks. Longhair cats are all the Persians, (including the Exotic Shorthair, as this is a breed with the Persian's looks, but just shorter hair). The Semi-longhairs are all the semi-longhaired breeds such as Birman, Maine Coon, and Turkish Van. The British group includes all the color variations of the British Shorthair, and also the Manx. Burmese is all the Burmese varieties. The Foreign section includes all the breeds that look "foreign" in type; that is, slender cats with long faces and rather tall ears, but not generally as exaggerated as a Siamese or Oriental. Thus, the Abyssinian belongs in this group, but so also do the Devon and Cornish Rexes, despite being native to Britain. The Oriental group include all the Oriental breeds—cats looking like Siamese in body and shape but of different colors. The Siamese group include all the Siamese varieties, as well as the Balinese.

In the US, many breeds of cat exist which have not yet reached the UK, or which are not accepted by the UK's largest cat registry, the Governing Council of the Cat Fancy, such as the Scottish Fold, the Nebelung, the Pixiebob, and the Munchkin. Therefore, for the purpose of this book, the different breeds have been segregated into the following groups which in no way are official:

Longhair breeds
Semi-longhair breeds
Shorthair breeds
Burmese and Foreign breeds
Siamese and Oriental breeds
Rex-coated breeds
Other breeds

The Tiffanie is the semi-longhaired variety of the Asian cat.

Cat Registries

To clarify which registries recognize each breed, the initials of the relevant organization(s) will be seen in brackets next to the breed names (see below).

Cat Registries

In the US, there are no less than six major cat registering bodies. These are (in alphabetical order):

AACE   American Association of Cat Enthusiasts
ACA   American Cat Association
ACFA   American Cat Fanciers' Association
CFA   Cat Fanciers' Association
CFF   Cat Fanciers' Federation
TICA   The International Cat Association

Each publishes a set of breed standards (detailing which breeds are recognized by them, and what the ideal show specimen of each cat should look like), organizes shows, etc. What can be rather confusing is that sometimes the different registries recognize different names for the same breed of cat; hence a FlamePoint Siamese is known as a Siamese within some registries, but as a Colorpoint Shorthair within others, and a long-haired Scottish Fold is known as a Highland Fold within certain organizations!

In the UK, the major registering group is the Governing Council of the Cat Fancy (GCCF), which also is the world's oldest registry for cats. The GCCF registers the great majority of pedigree cats in the UK, and grants licenses to most shows. There is also a much smaller organization, the Cat Association of Britain (CA), which is affiliated to the international group FIFe—*Fédération Internationale Feline*, and follows their rules.

The number of actual pedigree breeds of cat is much smaller in the UK than in the US. Many American breeds have yet not reached the UK, and some probably never will. Within the GCCF, it often takes as long as ten years for a new breed to be fully recognized and gain championship status (that is, cats of the breed in question being able to attain the title of Champion at shows), and so it takes very dedicated breeders indeed for any new breed to be recognized. Also, the GCCF employs very strict rules regarding cats' health, and it refuses to recognize certain breeds on the ground of health; for instance, it will not recognize the Munchkin with its short legs, or the Sphynx with its lack of fur.

Names of actual breeds, and also descriptions of colors, often vary between the two countries. The Himalayan Persian is known as the Colourpoint Persian in the UK and the rest of the world, the color Lilac is sometimes known as Lavender in the US, and so on.

The Semi-longhair Birman is popular throughout the world. As with many breeds classification varies slightly from country to country. In Britain it is preferred that the profile shows a slight dip, while in the US a curved, Roman profile is favored.

The look of the different breeds do at times also vary between the US and the UK. The Persian and Exotic breeds are generally much more extreme in looks in the US; with a much flatter face and cobbier body. The same look is not accepted by the GCCF, although many UK breeders do breed their cats to the US style. The Burmese has a different body shape in the US, and some US registries even divide the breed into two: American Burmese and European Burmese.

Cat Shows

Cat shows can attract thousands of entrants, and competition is fierce for titles. Even if you don't win, the shows are an excellent place to meet other cat enthusiasts. The picture shows a British cat show where the cats are individually penned for judging.

There is a very large difference in how cat shows are organized in the US and the UK. In the US, cats are generally shown in judging rings; each judge resides in a ring and will have the cats brought to him or her by the owner for examination, and the same cat can be judged by several different judges on the same day, or even over an entire weekend, and may be able to gain titles such as Champion in just one or two shows. To be able to gain titles, cats have to accumulate points, which are awarded according to how highly the cat is placed amongst all a particular judge's entrants in one ring. When not in the judging ring, each cat is caged in a large show pen, and these pens are lavishly decorated. There are no veterinary examinations necessary for the cats to be able to enter the show hall, and the exhibitors are able to exhibit their cats as often as they like.

In the UK, under the GCCF, the cats are judged in one main breed class, known as the open class, and can only be entered into one open class per show. If adult, the judge may award the winner of the open class a Challenge Certificate, and three such certificates (CCs) awarded by three different judges makes the cat a Champion. Each cat is caged in a pen which must be furnished all in white, and the exhibitors are not allowed inside the show hall whilst judging is in progress. The judges move from pen to pen with a judging table on wheels, and the cats do not need to be transported. The GCCF has a rule which states that no exhibitor may show any of their cats (even different cats) more frequently than every fourteen days, to minimize the risk of disease spreading at shows. Before even being allowed into the show hall, each cat is examined by a veterinary surgeon.

Cat Breeds

Longhair Cats

The only true Longhair cats are the Persian varieties and the gossamer-like coat of the Persian is its crowning glory.

The only true Longhair cats are the different Persian varieties—only they have the very full coat that is required for a pedigree cat to be titled Longhair. All other breeds with long fur, such as Birman and Maine Coon, are Semi-longhairs (see page 42), have coats of a different length and texture from the Persian coat. Confusingly, the Exotic Shorthair is also considered to be a longhair breed, despite its short coat. This is because the Exotic shares the general body shape of the Persian; it is a Persian cat with short fur.

The various Persian breeds all exhibit the same shape of body, known as type. The cat is medium to large in size, with cats as big as possible often being preferred by breeders and judges. The body is, however, moderate in length; the cat should be compact and feel heavy in comparison to its size. The legs are comparatively short and they should be very sturdy, with round paws. The tail is slightly shorter than in most other breeds. The head is perhaps the most obvious feature of the Persian cat: this should be very round with a perfectly flat profile. It should be possible to draw a vertical line from the Persian's forehead, onto the nose and down to the chin. The nose is generally placed either in between the eyes, at the same level, or just below eye level. The eyes are large and should be as round as possible, set well apart. The ears are small with rounded tips, and again should be spaced well apart, with a rounded top to the head, like a dome.

A Persian in full coat is a spectacular sight. The coat should be long all over the body, and stand out slightly from the body as opposed to hanging flatly down. There is a full neck ruff which should frame the face, and the fur on the tail should be at least long enough to be as wide as the body when brushed out like a fan. Needless to say, the Persian requires a great deal of grooming, and is not a breed suited for those uninterested in such a task. An ungroomed Persian soon becomes badly matted, and if the coat is left untended for any length of time, shaving the coat off is often the only option. The Persian's coat often changes with the weather, and so will be much fuller during colder periods—although if kept indoors with central heating the coat will not be noticeably fuller during cold

Right: This is a beautiful Pewter Persian.

Below: The Exotic Shorthair is the shorthaired variety of the Persian. As such, some registries still classify it as a longhair cat.

winter months. Some Persians never reach a full-length coat, but will still require a good amount of grooming as the coat may still mat due to its texture.

Persians and Exotics come in a very large variety of colors and markings; around 100 in total. The most popular ones include the selfs (all one color) such as Blue, Cream, White, Black, etc., the Bi-color (with white markings), Tabbies (in particular Brown Tabby, Silver Tabby, and Red Tabby), Smokes (cats with a white undercoat and darker coloring on top), Chinchilla (silver), Tortoiseshells (the classic red and black mix or other variations such as Blue Cream) and of course the ever-popular Himalayan (known as the Colourpoint outside the US)—the Persian with Siamese markings.

Above: The Chinchilla is an extremely popular, and very attractive, Persian variety.

Persian

(AACE, ACA, ACFA, CFA, CFF, TICA, GCCF, CA)

The Persian is one of the best-known breeds of pedigree cats, with a large worldwide popularity. The model Persian type is described on page 30, although there are variations in the breed standards—Persians with a slightly longer face are very common in the UK, for example. The rather exaggerated flatness of the facial features has not always been as evident in the breed as now. In former days the Persian had a longer face similar to that seen in semi-longhair cats, although the breed standard has always called for a short face and this is what selective breeding over the years has achieved.

The Persian developed naturally in the mountain regions of Persia, where the rough climate meant that any cat living wild had to have a long, dense coat to be able to survive. It has been known since the first-ever cat shows were staged in the 1800s, and now comes in around 100 different color variations. The temperament is placid, easygoing, and friendly.

Above: Bi-colored Persians such as these have only been accepted as a pattern fairly recently.

Left: The Persian is accepted in around 100 colors and patterns. This is a Cream Persian.

Above: Seal Point Himalayan. This attractive breed was formed by crossing Persians and Siamese.

Himalayan

(AACE, ACFA, CFF, TICA. Recognized as a Persian variety by the ACA, CFA, and GCCF)

The Himalayan is known as the Colourpoint Persian in countries outside the US. The breed was developed in the 1950s by crossing Persians and Siamese together, to achieve a Persian cat with the Persian type, but with the Siamese's striking colors. Interestingly, breeders in the US and the UK had independently strived to develop this breed, with the UK beating the US by a few years, and this is the reason for the breed being known by two different names.

The Himalayan is a Persian in every sense of the word, with the compact, heavy body and the flat face, together with the long coat that does not lie flat. No less than 20 different colors exist in the Himalayan breed, known as different "points." The Himalayan cat has a pale body, with darker-colored face mask, ears, legs, and tail. The eyes are always blue.

Temperament-wise, the Himalayan is as friendly and easygoing as the Persian, but is perhaps slightly more outgoing and playful.

Kashmir
(CFF)

The Kashmir is not a different breed as such; it is a Persian cat bred from a Himalayan parent, yet without the Himalayan's darker points on face, legs, and tail. When breeding a Himalayan to a Persian of other colors, the resulting kittens will not be pointed Himalayans, but will instead carry the gene for pointing. If mated to another carrier (known as a Colorpoint Carrier or CPC) or to a Himalayan, these cats will produce both pointed and non-pointed kittens. Most registries simply consider these cats to be Persians, although some Kashmirs do not make as good show specimens as Persians without Himalayan ancestry, as the Himalayan genes often serve to dilute the eye color of these cats. However, within the CFF these cats are registered as Kashmirs, and are treated as a separate breed.

In looks and temperament, there is nothing to distinguish the Kashmir from any other Persian; indeed, it is not possible to look at a cat and tell just from its looks that it is a Kashmir and not a Persian.

Above: Self Chocolate Kashmir. This is not a breed in its own right but a Persian that carries the gene for point markings.

Above: A Tortie and White Pekefaced Persian. The exaggeration of this breed's type does not cause any health problems but special care should be paid to cleaning the folds of skin around the eyes and nose when grooming.

Pekefaced Persian
(CFF)

The Pekefaced Persian is a Persian with an extremely exaggerated type; the face is reminiscent of that of a Pekingese dog, hence its name. This breed has existed for several decades, and in the beginning the Pekeface was vastly different from all other Persians, which were far less exaggerated in type. However, as the quality of Persians has improved by selective breeding over the years, the differences between the Pekeface and the ordinary Persian are now less obvious. However, the Pekeface exhibits some qualities which would be considered faults in the ordinary Persian, such as layers of folded skin underneath the eyes, a forehead with a markedly outward curve, a skull depression, and a wrinkled muzzle. The nose is extremely short, with large, prominent eyes. In every other respect, the Pekeface is a Persian, with the usual Persian features and temperament. The Pekefaced Persian is always Red or Red Tabby.

Exotic Shorthair
(AACE, ACA, ACFA, CFA, CFF, TICA, GCCF, CA)

The Exotic Shorthair is the shorthaired version of the Persian—the ideal cat for those who like the looks of the Persian cat with its appealing flat face, yet feel they cannot cope with the large amount of grooming required to keep a Persian's coat in good condition. The Exotic Shorthair originally came about as a by-product. Breeders in the US had crossed Persians to their American Shorthairs in order to introduce new blood and improve the type of their shorthairs. The resulting kittens were so different in type and coat that several breeders decided to embark upon a breeding program, and the result was named the Exotic Shorthair. This was in the 1960s. In the UK breeders of British Shorthairs discovered similar kittens when crossing their shorthairs to Persians in the early 1980s.

The Exotic Shorthair has all the Persian looks bar one: the coat. The Exotic is a heavy and compact cat, medium to large in size, with short, sturdy legs and a medium-length tail which must have a rounded tip. The head is round with a perfectly flat profile, the eyes large and round, the ears small, rounded, and set well apart. The coat is unlike the coat of any other shorthaired cats; it is of medium length (yet must never be as long as to flow like a semi-longhair's) and is so dense that it stands out slightly

Above: Blue Tabby Exotic Shorthairs. These cats are ideal pets for those that like the "kittenish" look of the Persian but do not have time for extensive grooming.

Right: Chocolate Exotic Shorthair.
Like the Persian these cats are very
contented and devoted pets with an
even, docile temperament.

from the body; it is important that the Exotic's coat never lies flat. The Exotic's coat requires slightly more grooming than that of an American Shorthair, for instance, yet it is still a breed that requires much less grooming than true longhairs. The Exotic Shorthair comes in all the color variations of the Persian. The temperament is friendly and mild-natured, but the Exotic is much more outgoing and playful than the Persian.

Exotic Longhair
(AACE, ACA, ACFA, CFF)

The Exotic Longhair is not, strictly speaking, an actual breed of cat; rather it is a by-product of Exotic Shorthair breeding. Some cat registries simply classify it as a Persian, and others as an Exotic Variant, which cannot be shown. As the Exotic Shorthair breed was developed by crossing Persian cats to shorthairs (American Shorthairs and British Shorthairs in the US and UK respectively) it was inevitable that all the early Exotic Shorthairs carried the gene for long fur, and so in most litters both shorthaired and longhaired kittens would be born. It is also very much standard practice to mate Exotic Shorthairs and Persians together, to improve the type of the Exotic, and to add new bloodlines to this comparatively rare breed. Homozygous Exotic Shorthairs do exist; that is, Exotics that do not carry the longhair gene and therefore will only produce shorthair kittens, but these are still the minority.

An Exotic Longhair cat cannot visibly be told apart from a Persian. Nor will it give different results when breeding to a pure Persian, as the gene for short fur cannot be carried, and therefore two longhair cats cannot produce shorthaired offspring. It is only by looking at the cat's pedigree that anyone can find out if it is indeed a Persian or an Exotic Longhair, as the Exotic Longhair will have shorthaired ancestors. This is also the reason for why some registries do not consider them to be pure Persians.

Above: Black and White Exotic Longhair. The Exotic Longhair comes in all the same colors as the Persian and Exotic Shorthair, and the temperament is the same as that of the Exotic Shorthair.

Semi-longhair Cats

Semi-longhairs—such as the Ragamuffin and Maine Coon—are among the biggest and heaviest breeds there are.

Semi-longhair cats are cats with a long coat, yet not of such fullness as the Persian and its variants. Whereas the Persian's coat will have a fluffed-up appearance, being of a woolly texture, and not lie flat, the semi-longhair coat lies smooth on the body, and has a somewhat coarser texture, with a much larger amount of heavy guard hairs. The coat will be comparatively short on the body itself, but the semi-longhair breeds will show a neck ruff, "trousers" on their hind legs, and a bushy tail. Most semi-longhairs share the trait that their coat will be at its fullest during cold winter months, with a very large neck ruff, in particular, a being evident. In warmer weather, the cat will often look almost shorthaired, with the exception of the slightly fluffy tail. For cats that live indoors in warm houses all year, the coat may never reach its full potential. The semi-longhair type of coat is the original longhair coat, which was developed naturally in cats living in colder climates, such as the mountain regions of Turkey, and also Scandinavia. The coat does not mat as easily as that of the Persian, and it should be weatherproof; not allowing any wetness to seep in close to the skin.

The various semi-longhair breeds vary in looks, with two of the most popular, the Maine Coon and the Ragdoll, also being the two largest breeds known of pedigree cats. Others are medium in size. Most semi-longhairs show a moderate body shape without any exaggerations; an altogether natural-looking cat. The body will be fairly long with average length legs and a long tail, the head moderate in shape, sometimes with a slight nose break. The ears are of medium size, the eyes usually almond-shaped.

The semi-longhair pedigree cat is often one of an even disposition; a playful cat without being overly energetic, yet not placid like the Persian. Obviously, there are temperament differences between the various breeds found in this group, with the Ragdoll in particular being known as a placid cat.

Grooming the semi-longhair coat is much easier than grooming the Persian coat. A weekly grooming session is enough for most semi-longhairs, as the coat is not prone to mat or tangle; when the coat is at its shortest during the summer it will be an easy task indeed. The areas to pay particular attention to will be behind the ears, the neck ruff, on the stomach, and the "trousers" on the hind legs.

Above: Blue Point Birmans. The distinctive semi-longhaired coat is very silky and flows across the body. A ruff flows from the neck, the back legs have "breeches," and the tail is fully plumed.

Birman

The Birman is a very popular breed of cat worldwide, thought to have similar origins to those of the Siamese. The Birman was a naturally occurring cat and not a breed created by man; that is, apart from the different colorings which breeders developed over several years. The breed first reached France from Asia in 1919, but did not spread to other countries until decades later.

The Birman is a semi-longhaired cat of striking beauty. The cat's body is pale, almost white, with a darker face mask, ears, legs, and tail. On the front legs, the cat shows white "gloves," and the hind legs have larger white "gauntlets." The eyes are always a vivid blue. The coat is semi-long and silky, being at its fullest on the cat's chest, hind legs, and tail. No less than 20 colors of the Birman exist, known as "points." The Birman is a medium-sized cat with no exaggerations. It is sweet-natured, outgoing, friendly, and playful.

Above: Seal Point Birmans. The Birman comes in the traditional Siamese (Himalayan) pattern in a complete range of colors, but the most dramatic feature is the characteristic white feet.

Left: Cream Point Birman. Cats of this breed are extremely loyal and playful pets and will "talk" to their owner in a gentle, low voice.

Above: Maine Coon (lying down) with an Oriental Tortie companion. This is an old and natural breed that some believe was brought to the US in Viking longboats centuries before Columbus discovered America.

Maine Coon
(AACE, ACA, ACFA, CFA, CFF, TICA, GCCF, CA)

The Main Coon is a naturally occurring cat, which was possibly originally brought to Maine by the Vikings. The Maine Coon is a very large and heavy cat, with a weather-resistant coat designed to make the cat able to survive outdoors even in the roughest of climates. In cold weather, the Maine Coon will sport a heavy coat with a particularly large neck ruff and bushy tail; in warmer weather the coat will look almost like that of a shorthaired breed. The head is somewhat square with tall ears, the neck very broad, and the entire cat is muscular and powerful. The Maine Coon comes in all colors with the exception of Himalayan pattern, Chocolate or Lilac, with tabbies being the most popular varieties; a tabby Maine Coon gives the impression of an entirely wild-looking cat.

The Maine Coon can reach an adult weight of up to 25 lb, and the breed is often said to be dog-like, with the cats becoming devoted companions to their owners, and liking games such as retrieving small toys.

Norwegian Forest Cat
(AACE, ACA, ACFA, CFA, CFF, TICA, GCCF, CA)

The Norwegian Forest Cat is somewhat similar to the Maine Coon; for many years it was virtually unknown outside the Scandinavian countries, whereas the Maine Coon was popular only in the US. For many years the Norwegian Forest Cat was never bred by man but continuing to exist as a natural breed in the wilds of its native Norway. It was not until the 1970s that breeders started a controlled breeding program of the Norwegian Forest Cat, as it was then close to extinction.

The coat of the Norwegian Forest Cat is dense and water-resistant, much heavier in the winter than in the summer. The cat is of medium to large size, with an entirely natural-looking body. The face is not as square as that of the Maine Coon, but shows similar tall ears with ear tufts. The Norwegian Forest Cat comes in any color or pattern, with the one exception of the Himalayan pattern which is not accepted. In particular, tabbies and black, white, or black and white cats are popular.

The Norwegian Forest Cat is an independent cat which often attaches itself to one person in the family, to whom it will be very loyal.

Above: Originating from the wild, harsh climate of Scandinavia, the Norwegian Forest Cat has dense fur with a thick, wooly undercoat. Owners of Norwegian Forest Cats should be careful that their pet does not become too accustomed to warm surroundings as this will impair the beautiful, thick coat.

Above: Blue Point Mitted Ragamuffin. This is an extremely friendly breed of cat that is famous for its excellent temperament.

Ragamuffin
(ACFA)

The Ragamuffin is essentially the same breed as the Ragdoll, but of colors other than those recognized in the Ragdoll breed. The creator of the Ragdoll trademarked the breed name "Ragdoll," and sold franchises in the breed to interested breeders. After years of being supervised, several breeders decided to leave and start breeding on their own. They then decided to limit their Ragdoll breeding to four basic colors, and the breed was eventually recognized by most of the major cat registries. In the meantime, other breeders were still continuing to breed the original Ragdoll cat, which was not limited colorwise. In 1994, another group of breeders left the original group, and as they could no longer register their cats as Ragdolls, being of the wrong colors, they decided to call their version of the breed Ragamuffin.

Like Ragdolls, Ragamuffins are among the biggest and heaviest breeds there are. The body is natural in shape, neither sleek nor cobby. The coat can be of any color, and can be either Bi-color (with white markings), Mitted (white paws only) or without any white markings.

What is most important in a Ragamuffin is its temperament, and dedicated breeders have made sure that this is a very friendly, loyal, and outgoing breed of cat.

Ragdoll

(AACE, ACFA, CFA, CFF, TICA, GCCF, CA)

The Ragdoll is a breed surrounded by controversy. For years it was claimed that this was a breed of cat unable to feel pain, and originally it was being marketed as the ideal pet cat as here was a breed that would never defend itself, even if hurt. The breed originated in California, and the woman who founded the breed and even trademarked it, claimed that the original queen had been brain-damaged due to an accident, and as such was unable to feel any pain. When this queen had kittens, it was said that all her kittens showed the same unusual traits. This is, of course, a genetic impossibility, and it has since been scientifically proved that the Ragdoll is no different from any other breed of cat

The Ragdoll is a very large cat, often said to be the largest pedigree breed. It is heavy and muscular, but without any exaggerations in body or type. The coat is semi-long and at its fullest on the chest and tail. The Ragdoll comes in just four different colors—Seal, Blue, Lilac, and Chocolate Colorpointed, all pointed Himalayan-pattern cats with blue eyes. It can also be Mitted (with white paws) or Bi-color. It is a friendly and loyal cat which avoids conflict.

Above: A Bi-color Blue Ragdoll. Due to their extremely equable and docile temperament it was rumored that Ragdolls could feel no pain. However, these cats are normal in every respect and should be given the same respect and care as any other breed.

Right: A Silver Tortie Siberian. These cats have long, plumed tails and manes that develop from the back of the head, sweeping down to the chest. Their coats are dense, soft, and very velvety.

Siberian

(AACE, ACA, ACFA, CFF, TICA)

Siberia is rather an unusual origin for a pedigree breed of cat. The breed is naturally occurring, and parallels can be drawn with breeds such as the Maine Coon. There was no such thing as an organized Russian cat fancy until the 1980s, but when it was formed this native breed, the Siberian, started to become noticed in various other countries, including the US. The Siberian has not, however, reached Great Britain.

The Siberian is quite a big cat, without any exaggerations, showing an altogether natural-looking body, although the face is perhaps a shade longer than that of the average non-pedigree cat.

There are no color restrictions in the Siberian breed; all colors and markings, including the pointed Himalayan pattern, are acceptable. It is a natural cat both in looks and behavior, neither placid and laid back, nor particularly vocal or energetic.

Somali

(AACE, ACA, ACFA, CFA, CFF, TICA, GCCF, CA)

The Somali can be described as a semi-longhaired Abyssinian. For years, Abyssinian breeders had found longhair kittens born into their litters, and in the UK these kittens were sold off cheaply as pets, not to be bred from, as they were considered to be Abyssinians "gone wrong." In the US, however, the Abyssinian breeders realized the potential for a new breed when finding longhaired kittens in their litters, and started a controlled breeding program to increase the numbers of these longhairs. The new breed, named the Somali, thus existed in the US for years before interested breeders in the UK decided to import breeding cats—it was not until 1980 that the first Somalis were imported from America into Britain.

The Somali is a cat of Foreign type, yet it is normally classified as a semi-longhair breed. It has a moderately long head and tall ears, and is of medium size and slender in build.

In color, the Somali is always Ticked Tabby, a tabby cat without any stripes except for the usual "M" marking on the forehead. The various Somali colors are the same as seen in the Abyssinian. The two original and most common colors are Ruddy (known as Usual in the UK), a ruddy orange/apricot color with black ticking, and Sorrel, which is of a redder shade, with the black ticking being less obvious.

Above: Ruddy (Usual) Somali. The Somali is a playful and energetic cat, friendly and always ready for a game.

Turkish Van
(AACE, ACFA, CFA, CFF, TICA, GCCF, CA)
The Turkish Van is believed to have existed as a breed for hundreds of years, originating from the Lake Van area of Turkey. It was unknown outside Turkey until 1955, when a British journalist traveling through Turkey came across the Van cats by chance.

The Turkish Van is a natural-looking semi-longhair cat, with a slightly longer head than average. The breed is fairly large, and many Turkish Vans are much heavier than they look.

The most distinguishing feature of the breed is its unusual markings: white with colored patches around each ear and a colored tail. Some specimens show one or more patches of color on the body as well, but this is undesirable. The classic Turkish Van can be either Auburn or Cream, with amber, blue, or odd-colored eyes. The most common color is Auburn with amber eyes. Other colors of the Turkish Van have recently been bred, for instance with Tortoiseshell markings instead of Auburn or Cream. In order to achieve this, the breed was outcrossed to other breeds, something which had never before been done. Accordingly, most Turkish Van breeders do not consider these Van-patterned to be proper Turkish Vans, as they are no longer purebred.

York Chocolate

(ACFA, CFF)

The York Chocolate originated in New York only in the 1980s. A semi-longhaired black and white non-pedigree cat gave birth to a litter of kittens which included one that was chocolate brown. Eventually more and more chocolate-colored kittens started to appear from the same family of cats, and their owner embarked upon a controlled breeding program.

This is a large breed of cat, muscular yet with a lean body. It has a long face, tall ears, and long legs. The York Chocolate comes in four different color variations: Chocolate, Chocolate and White Bi-color, Lavender, and Lavender and White. There are also Van-patterned cats, with the same markings as the Turkish Van.

The York Chocolate is an energetic and very playful cat, loving and friendly.

Above: Chocolate and White York Chocolate. Cats of this breed have an extremely graceful bearing and very lithe, flexible bodies.

Burmese and Foreign Breeds

Burmese cats are very popular, a breed somewhere between the Siamese and the American Shorthair. Cats described as "foreign" in looks are slender cats with svelte bodies and fairly long faces, yet without any of the exaggerations seen in breeds such as the Siamese or the Oriental. What can be confusing at times is the fact that many breeds are described as foreign despite being native to the country in question—such as the Cornish and Devon Rex in the UK. For the purpose of this book, however, all the different rex breeds have been grouped together under their own breed heading (see page 104).

Needless to say, here we find a number of very different breeds. Whereas the Burmese is similar in temperament to its descendant the Tonkinese and also the Asian breeds, it is nothing like breeds such as the Abyssinian. It is therefore impossible to generalize about the temperament and behavior of the breeds grouped together here.

Most Burmese and Foreign cats have very short and sleek coats. As such, they require very little grooming. The cats themselves do an excellent job of keeping the coat in good condition by licking themselves carefully many times a day, and as long as the cat is fed on a good quality diet, the coat should stay smooth, shiny, and healthy-looking. The only grooming necessary will be a weekly brushing with a soft-bristled brush. The semi-longhair breeds here, such as the Tiffanie (see under Asian), will require slightly more coat care, but again the actual grooming process is minimal. A weekly brushing and combing session with a fine-toothed metal comb and a soft-bristled brush is all that is needed.

Chocolate Burmese kitten.

Above: These Ruddy (Usual) Abyssinian kittens will grow into balanced, medium-sized cats of Foreign type with a well ticked close-lying coat.

Abyssinian

(AACE, ACA, ACFA, CFA, CFF, TICA, GCCF, CA)

The Abyssinian may have derived from the Egyptian hunting cat, but the exact origins of the breed are unknown. It is a very old breed of cat, certainly dating back to the nineteenth century.

The Abyssinian is a cat of Foreign type, medium in size. It is slender but not cobby. The coat is short, and always Ticked Agouti, i.e. a Tabby cat without any actual stripes other than on the forehead. The two most common colors of the Abyssinian is the Ruddy (known as Usual in the UK) and the Sorrel. The Ruddy Abyssinian is of a reddish orange to apricot color, evenly ticked with black. The Sorrel is a much redder shade, where the black ticking is less obvious. There are several other colors available as well.

The Abyssinian is friendly and outgoing, a curious and intelligent cat.

Above: A Red (Sorrel) Abyssinian kitten. The color of this kitten is already noticably more red than that of the kitten on the far left.

Left: The Fawn is one of the newer, dilute colors of Abyssinian.

Above: Available in a wide variety of colors and patterns, the Asians have a soft, silky coat.

Asian
(GCCF)

The Asian is in fact several different breeds, amongst which the Burmilla probably is the best known. When the Burmilla was created, quite by accident, other colors and also coat lengths appeared, and these became the different types of Asian cat. The breeds originate from a litter born by accident in 1981, with a Chinchilla Persian father and a Burmese mother. The Asian breeds are virtually unknown outside the UK.

Broadly speaking, the Asian breeds are Burmese-type cats of colors not found in the Burmese breed. The group includes the Burmilla, which is Silver-colored Burmese; the Asian Smoke, a non-agouti silvered cat; the Asian Tabby; the Asian Selfs, which include the Bombay; and the Tiffanie, which is the semi-longhair of the group.

Bengal

(ACA, ACFA, CFF, TICA, GCCF, CA)

The Bengal was deliberately created to resemble a wild cat. This was achieved by mating the small Asian leopard cat with domestic pet cats in the US. There is only a very small amount of wild blood in the Bengal breed today, and the main differences between the Bengal and other domestic breeds are therefore mainly in looks and not in temperament.

A very muscular, large cat, the Bengal should as far as possible look like a true wild cat. The body is sleek and powerful, the hind legs slightly longer than the front legs. The head is broad and slightly rounded. The coat is very thick and soft. The coloring is always Spotted or Marble Tabby, and can be either Brown Marbled, Snow Marbled, Brown Spotted, or Snow Spotted. The markings are better defined than in other Tabby cats, and the Spotteds have larger spots. The coat has an almost satinized appearance, known as glitter.

The Bengal must be a friendly and reliable cat, with no hint of wildness in its temperament.

Above: The Snow Spotted Bengal reflects the look of a wild snow leopard.

Right: Nicknamed "the patent leather kid with copper penny eyes," the Bombay is essentially a Burmese cat with a solid black coat.

Bombay
(ACA, ACFA, CFA, CFF, TICA, GCCF)
The Bombay is essentially a black Burmese, and was created by crossing Burmese to black cats. In the US, the first crosses were made to black American Shorthairs, in the UK to black non-pedigree cats. The Bombay is always Black.

Due to its ancestry, the Bombay has a similar body and build to the Burmese, and in the UK it counts as one of the Asian breeds. The Burmese is not as sleek and svelte as the Siamese, nor is it as rounded as the American Shorthair; the body and facial features are rather somewhere in between the two. The Bombay is medium in size, with a sleek coat. The jet black color is always accompanied by yellow or green eyes.

Behaviorwise, the Bombay is a lively, playful, and outgoing breed, a cat which loves the company of people and other cats, and which always is ready for a game.

Burmese

(AACE, ACA, ACFA, CFA, CFF, TICA, GCCF, CA)

The first Burmese arrived in the US in 1920. The breed originated in Thailand, alongside the Siamese, and is believed to have occurred naturally for many hundreds of years.

The Burmese is an elegant cat, with a head more rounded than that of its cousin, the Siamese. The body is slender but not at all as svelte as the Siamese body. It is medium in size, with a short and sleek coat. There are several differences between the US Burmese and the European counterpart (such as the shape of the head, which is more square in the US), so much so that certain registries even consider them to be two different breeds.

The Burmese has always been most popular in brown, where the coloring is a rich seal brown. The other colors found in the breed are Blue, Chocolate, Lilac, Red, Brown Tortie (tortoiseshell), Cream, Blue Tortie, Chocolate Tortie, and Lilac Tortie.

The Burmese is playful and curious, a lively and attentive cat that loves company and makes an excellent family pet.

Above: A Sable (Brown) Burmese. Cats of this breed are extremely playful and energetic and will seem to eat twice as much as any other breed due to their exertions!

Right: Breed conformation differs slightly between Burmese in the US and Great Britain but on both sides of the Atlanitic the coat is fine, glossy, satin-like texture, short, and very close-lying as can be seen in this beautiful example of the breed.

Left: A Lilac Burmese. Other popular colors include Blue, Chocolate, Red, Brown Tortie (tortoiseshell), Cream, Blue Tortie, Chocolate Tortie, and Lilac Tortie.

Right: Brown Tortie Burmese.

Chantilly
(AACE, ACFA)

The true origins of the Chantilly breed will probably never be fully known; the breed as it is today originated from a pair of chocolate-brown semi-longhaired cats of unknown background, purchased by a cat fancier from New York in 1967. During the 1970s these cats were registered by the ACA as Foreign Longhairs; later the breed name was changed to Tiffany. However, the ACA eventually dropped the breed from its register as there were not enough examples in existence. The breed was resurrected when it was found that it in fact existed in Canada, where it had appeared naturally, and some specimens were imported to the US. By this time there was a British breed known as the Tiffanie, so the name of this altogether different breed was changed yet again, this time to Chantilly.

The Chantilly is a cat with Foreign build and a medium-sized body. The coat is semi-long, with the longest fur being found on the chest and tail. The color is always chocolate brown.

The Chantilly is a friendly cat of a medium disposition; it is curious and outgoing, but not overly energetic, nor very placid.

Above: A Chantilly kitten already showing the semi-long coat that is characteristic of the breed.

Right: This Chantilly kitten shows the Brown coat that is the breed's trademark.

Egyptian Mau
(AACE, ACA, ACFA, CFA, CFF, TICA, CA)

The Egyptian Mau probably originates from Egypt, although the first Maus to have been documented were in fact owned by a Russian princess. Whilst living in Rome, the princess had been given an Egyptian Mau kitten as a gift. When she left Italy for the US in 1956 she brought with her three Egyptian Maus, which became the foundation for the breed in the US.

The Egyptian Mau is always a Spotted Tabby, with round spots of even size covering the entire body with the exception of the face, legs, and tail, which are striped as in any other tabby cat. The coat is short and lies flat. The body of the Egyptian Mau is comparatively large for a foreign breed. It is more rounded in appearance than an Oriental or Siamese, yet not as rounded as the American Shorthair. The breed comes in several different colors; for instance Bronze, Silver, and Smoke, with the spots being black or blue, depending upon the body color.

Early Egyptian Maus often had an unpredictable, sometimes even aggressive, temperament; something which was believed to be due to the possibility of wild ancestors. These days the Egyptian Mau is an even-tempered pet cat, which shows high intelligence, curiosity, and playfulness.

Above: As can be seen in this picture the Egyptian Mau has a medium length coat that is short and very sleek.

Right: The Korat is a particularly attractive breed that has beautiful green eyes. The silver tipping on its coat gives a wonderful sheen to its appearance.

Korat
(AACE, ACA, ACFA, CFA, CFF, TICA, GCCF, CA)
The Korat is a very old breed which originated in Thailand hundreds of years ago, alongside the Siamese and other similar breeds. The Korat may have existed in the UK in the late 1800s, but records are unclear. Officially the breed did not reach the US until 1959, and the UK in 1972.

Having never been outcrossed to other breeds, the Korat should still look exactly the same today as the breed did when it first developed hundreds of years ago. A centuries-old poem gives a description of the Korat which still could be used to describe the breed as it is known today. The best-known feature of the Korat is perhaps its head, which has an unusual heart shape. The eyes are very large and green in color. The body is medium in size but still feels heavy, the coat short and sleek. The color of the Korat is blue with silver tips to each hair, which give the coat a silver sheen.

The Korat is an intelligent breed which craves company. A friendly and playful breed, the Korat often attaches itself to one person in particular.

Nebelung

(CFF, TICA)

The Nebelung is essentially a semi-longhair version of the Russian Blue, and it is believed to have existed as early as the 1800s. The breed then disappeared, presumably due to lack of interested breeders, and it did not reappear until the 1980s, when the first modern-day Nebelungs were registered in the US. The breed has the Russian Blue as its ancestor, and the two breeds look very similar, with the obvious exception of the coat length. The Nebelung is not seen in the UK.

The Nebelung is an elegant-looking Foreign breed, with a long body and light boning. It is a comparatively small cat, although some specimens may be medium-sized. The head is fairly long with a straight nose. The coat is semi-long, soft to the touch, and glossy. The color of the Nebelung is always blue, and each blue hair shows a silver tip.

The Nebelung is loyal and loving toward its owner, but does not tend to greet strangers with enthusiasm, being a rather shy cat. It is highly intelligent and curious.

Above: A Nebelung showing the classic blue coat with silver tipping.

Right: Ocicat kittens have a delightful sense of mischief that will endure all their lives.

Ocicat
(AACE, ACA, ACFA, CFA, CFF, TICA, GCCF, CA)
The Ocicat was created to look like a wild cat, but unlike the somewhat similar Bengal, no wild blood has ever been introduced into the Ocicat. The breed originated in the US in the 1960s from Abyssinian crosses. Ocicats are medium in size, and must be muscular and powerful, slender but not at all slim. The head is of medium length.

The Ocicat is always Spotted Tabby and shorthaired. The spotting is what gives the Ocicat its unique looks, and so the color and markings are being paid a great deal of attention by dedicated breeders; the spots must be distinct and clear. The Ocicat can be of many different colors, such as Silver, Chocolate, Sorrel, Blue, Fawn, etc.

The Ocicat is curious, intelligent, and friendly, an outgoing and playful cat which makes an excellent pet.

Russian Blue

(AACE, ACA, ACFA, CFA, CFF, TICA, GCCF, CA)

The Russian Blue breed is a very old breed of cat which originated in Russia, but not many details are known as to how this elegant breed developed. The first Russian Blues to arrive in the UK were brought into the country by Russian sailors, and the breed is believed to have been exhibited at the first-ever cat show in 1871. It has remained a less popular breed than its bigger and heftier British counterpart, the British Blue. The Russian Blue is medium in size and of elegant Foreign type, slender but not as slim as an Oriental. The tall ears are set on a fairly long head.

The coat of the Russian Blue is short and thick but must not lie flat, due to it being so dense. As its name suggests, the Russian Blue is always Self Blue in color, and as each hair is tipped with silver it gives the impression of having a silver sheen.

The Russian Blue is an energetic and outgoing cat with a high level of intelligence and curiosity.

Above: A Russian Blue looking typically elegant. This ancient breed was originally known in Britain as the Archangel cat as it was thought to have been brought from Archangel in Russia by seafarers.

Right: Russian Blues are famous for having a wonderful temperament. Quiet and loving, these cats are completely devoted to their owners though they might sometimes like to enjoy their own company in a secluded spot that will quickly become their own territory.

Singapura

(AACE, ACA, ACFA, CFA, CFF, TICA, GCCF)

The Singapura may have developed as early as 300 years ago, in Singapore. It originates from crosses between various breeds of cat, and possibly wild cats as well. The breed existed in Singapore untouched by man for centuries, and it did not reach the US until the 1970s.

For a long time the Singapura was known as the smallest breed of pedigree cat; earning the nickname of "the drain cat"—as it was so small it could presumably fall down a drain! It is certainly a very small breed of cat compared to the majority of pedigree breeds, but these days the Singapura is not as minute as the first examples that were imported to the US; the original small size was more than likely caused by the cats suffering from poor nutrition. The Singapura's body is medium in every way without any exaggerations, and the coat is short. What makes the Singapura instantly recognizable from other breeds is its head, which looks small in comparison to the body, and shows very large, expressive eyes.

The Singapura is always Sepia Agouti in color, referred to as Brown Ticked Agouti outside the US. It is lively and playful yet not an extrovert, an athletic cat which loves jumping and climbing.

Above: The Singapura is only available in one color — Sepia Agouti — which is pale ivory with sepia brown ticking.

Tonkinese
(AACE, ACA, ACFA, CFA, CFF, TICA, GCCF)

The Tonkinese can most easily be described as a cross between a Siamese and a Burmese, with its looks truly being somewhere in between the two breeds. The Tonkinese was not bred within the cat fancy until the 1960s, but as both the Siamese and the Burmese originate from Thailand centuries ago, it is a fair assumption that early crosses had taken place, and so the Tonkinese may have been in existence for much longer.

The Tonkinese is a very attractive and unusual-looking cat. Like the Siamese, it has darker points to face, ears, legs, and tail, but the body is not pale cream or white in color but rather a paler shade of the points coloring. The body is long and slender, not as slim and fine as that seen in the Siamese, yet not as rounded as the Burmese's body either. The coat is always short and sleek, and comes in a variety of different colors.

The Tonkinese is friendly, always up to mischief, intelligent, and out-going, a cat which stays young at heart for all of its life.

Left: The coat of the Turkish Angora is medium long, silky, and fine and should be wavy on the stomach. A highly intelligent breed they will become bored if left on their own.

Turkish Angora
(AACE, ACA, ACFA, CFA, CFF, TICA, CA)

The original longhaired cat, the Turkish Angora developed naturally in the mountainous regions of Turkey, where the climate could be rough and very varied, so any cat living wild would need a thick and dense coat to be able to survive.

The Turkish Angora is semi-longhaired and shows Foreign type; a slender and graceful cat, with a long yet muscular body. The face is fairly long, but not as long as that of the otherwise very similar breed, the Longhaired Oriental. There is no nose break. The Turkish Angora has a coat which is fine and silky in texture, fairly short but fuller on the tail and the neck ruff.

The most popular color for the Turkish Angora has always been white, but other colors exist as well, and the breed is accepted in any color or pattern except for Chocolate, Lavender, or the pointed Himalayan pattern.

The Turkish Angora is a very energetic and playful breed of high intelligence, the sort of cat that easily becomes bored if left on its own for too long.

Shorthair Cats

Many of the shorthair cat breeds can perhaps best be described as "pedigree moggies." Breeds such as the American Shorthair, the British Shorthair, and the European Shorthair all originated as farm cats in their respective native countries—hardy, natural-looking cats kept as mousers. With the start of the formal cat fancy, many of these breeds were in danger of becoming extinct, as all supervised breeding concentrated on more exotic-looking cats such as Persians and Siamese, and when these new breeds started to mix freely with the native shorthaired cats, the look of the natural cat started to change. Breeders eventually realized the potential of the native cats, and started controlled breeding programs. In doing so, the cat's original looks were slightly altered: the American Shorthair took on a somewhat square appearance, while the British Shorthair became a large cat with a rounded face.

The shorthair breeds are all natural-looking with no exaggerations; there are no overly long or very short faces, no very slender bodies. The cats are sturdy and robust, with a short coat that requires very little grooming other than that carried out by the cat itself. A brushing once a week is usually sufficient for most shorthair breeds. The temperament does, of course, vary from breed to breed, but generally speaking shorthair breeds are very even-natured, friendly, and outgoing, perhaps not as forthcoming as some other breeds, but not shy or nervous in any way. Being the happy medium of cats, shorthair breeds tend to be playful when it suits them, having a lot of energy, but they are in no way extroverts. For many people, these are the ideal pet cats, as here we have friendly cats that are easy to handle, yet with the cat's typical independent nature. Shorthair cats do not mind being left on their own for part of the day; they will simply settle down for a rest. Being such natural cats, most shorthairs have a long lifespan and are hardy cats which seldom succumb to disease—although, of course, any cat of any breed can fall ill.

The one fact that sets the shorthair pedigree breeds apart from the average non-pedigree cat, is their color. Shorthair pedigree cats come in a very large variety of striking colors, including the Siamese "points.". The shorthair pedigree owner really does have the best of the two worlds: a natural-looking cat with no exaggerations, yet with a striking appearance in coat color.

A British Shorthair showing the Colorpointed pattern that is relatively new to this breed. Due to their Siamese ancestry, cats of this pattern are often more outgoing in personality than the self colors.

Above: American Silver Tabby. This is the most popular color for the breed although there are 80 different colors and patterns that are accepted by cat registries.

American Shorthair

(AACE, ACA, ACFA, CFA, CFF, TICA)

Records exist which state that there were cats on board the Mayflower when it sailed from Plymouth to the New World, and these cats may well have been the ancestors of the American Shorthair. This most natural-looking of breeds was one of the very first to be recognized as a pedigree breed in the US.

The American Shorthair is the type of cat that you might expect to go out and catch mice for a living. It is a refined pedigree breed, yet there is nothing delicate about the American Shorthair; it is a true house cat built to do the job that the first ever domesticated cats were kept to do: catch and kill vermin. The American Shorthair is medium to large in size, well-built, giving an impression of being strong and powerful. The head is large and rather square, more so than in most other shorthair breeds. The coat is short and dense, thick enough to be water-resistant, which makes it not as sleek as the coat of many other shorthair breeds.

The most commonly seen American Shorthair color is Silver Tabby, a very striking color. There are, however, as many as 80 colors accepted in the breed, the one exception being Himalayan patterned cats.

The American Shorthair is a cat with a reliable temperament, gentle and friendly and trustworthy, making an excellent pet. It tends to get particularly attached to one family member, to whom it will be very loyal, and may not greet strangers with enthusiasm.

British Shorthair

(AACE, ACA, ACFA, CFA, CFF, TICA, GCCF, CA)

The British Shorthair has been a recognized breed in the UK since the very beginning of the cat fancy, and is still a very popular breed of cat, both as a pet and a show animal.

The British Shorthair is large in size, a very rounded and teddybear-like cat. The head is round with very full apple cheeks, but the British Shorthair lacks the short nose seen in the Persian and Exotic breeds. It has a short and very dense coat and is a generally sturdy-looking cat.

The most popular color of the British Shorthair is the Self Blue, known as the British Blue. Blue is the color that has remained the most popular in the breed ever since the British Shorthair was first registered as a pedigree breed. There are now many other colors available, including the British Colourpointed (marked like a Siamese) and the very delicately colored British Tipped, which shows the same color as the Chinchilla Persian.

The British Shorthair is friendly and easygoing in temperament, and tends to get on with most other cats as well as dogs. Some specimens are true lap cats that love spending time dozing on their owner's lap; others are more independent.

Above: Lilac British Shorthair. As with the American Shorthair there are now many colors and patterns available.

Right: American Silver Tabby.

Above: British Silver Tabby.

Left: British Silver Tabbies are sometimes more finely boned than the self colors — especially the females.

Above: Chartreux cats are naturally occurring Shorthairs with very dense coats much like that of the British Shorthair. They are always blue in color.

Chartreux

(AACE, ACA, ACFA, CFA, CFF, TICA, CA)

The Chartreux is a very old breed of cat which originates from France. It is believed that it has been in existence since the sixteenth century.

Similar to the British Blue, the Chartreux is a very big cat, with the dense, short, water-repellent coat which makes it able to withstand most types of weather when living outdoors. The Chartreux is famous for it very broad head with apple cheeks. It has a medium-length nose without the flat profile of the Persian, with which it otherwise shares the rounded head type. The Chartreux is a strongly built cat, very robust and obviously built as a hunter able to catch not only rats and mice, but probably small rabbits as well.

The Chartreux is always blue in color; any shade from ash grey to slate blue, and the tips of each hair are silver, giving it a sparkling appearance.

As a breed, the Chartreux has a calm and steady temperament, a cat which does not get upset easily. Being fairly laid back, the Chartreux still enjoys games such as chasing small balls.

European Shorthair
(CA)

This is the only breed of cat that can count Sweden as its home country. The breed was first recognized in 1946, but this was then under the name of "Swedish Housecat." The name was later changed to European Shorthair.

The European Shorthair really is the pedigree moggy; a medium-sized cat with a well-muscled body completely devoid of any exaggerations. The head could be described as somewhat large in comparison to the body, and rounded, with a nose which is broad and of medium length. The cheeks are well-developed, but nowhere near as rounded as those seen in the British Shorthair or the Chartreux. The coat is dense and glossy.

The European Shorthair can be seen in most colors, with the exception of Chocolate, Lilac, Cinnamon, Fawn, or the pointed Himalayan pattern. In other words, the colors normally seen in non-pedigree cats.

The European Shorthair is a medium of a cat; there are no exaggerations either in body or behavior. A friendly, playful, and highly intelligent cat with a good nature.

Above: Black European Shorthair. This breed is found in many colors and patterns and the coat is short and dense with quite a crisp texture.

Above: Not all Manx cats are tailess, this is a "longie," meaning that it has a full tail and would be used only for breeding.

Manx

(AACE, ACA, ACFA, CFA, TICA, GCCF, CA)

There is a legend surrounding the Manx, saying that the Manx cats were the last animals to get on board the Ark, and as they were late their tails got shut in the door when it closed, and so were cut off. Ever since then, the Manx has lacked a tail. In reality, the Manx originates from the British Isle of Man, and is a very old breed of cat. Early written records state that it was believed to have come to the Isle of Man originally on Spanish vessels, part of the Spanish Armada in the 1500s.

When a Manx cat has no tail at all, it is referred to as being a "rumpy." Cats with part of a tail, known as "stumpies," and also Manx cats with full tails, "longies," are frequently born into Manx litters. The Manx has an unusually short back, with the hind legs longer than the front legs. This makes the Manx cat's gait somewhat rabbit-like. The Manx is medium in size, with a heavy body. The head is large and round with apple cheeks, the nose broad but straight. Essentially, the Manx looks like a British Shorthair minus the tail. The Manx also comes in all the same colors, with the exception of the pointed Colorpoint pattern.

The temperament of the Manx is easygoing and fearless, a cat of medium activity levels.

Above: The more familiar tailess Manx cat.

Left: The Manx has an shorter back than most other breeds and its hind legs are longer than its front legs.

Above: The Snowshoe is famous for its unusual coloring. This is a Chocolate Point.

Snowshoe

(AACE, ACA, ACFA, CFF, TICA)

The Snowshoe was created by crossing Siamese, Oriental Shorthair, and American Shorthairs together; it originated in the US in the 1960s.

The Snowshoe is heavy without looking too solid, a cat of medium size and build in all parts of the body. The most famous feature of the Snowshoe is its unusual coloring: Siamese pattern combined with white markings. The white markings vary between individuals, with some cats being more heavily marked than others. Similar to the Ragdoll, the Snowshoe can be either Mitted, where the only white markings are to be found on the paws, or Bi-color, where there is also white on the face and chest. The points coloring can be either Seal, Blue, Chocolate, Lilac, Cinnamon, or Fawn, although Seal Point and Blue Point are the two most popular color varieties. As in all pointed cats, the eyes of the Snowshoe are always blue.

The Snowshoe is a very affectionate and intelligent cat, which craves company.

Left: Like all Pointed cats the Snowshow has vivid blue eues.

Siamese and Oriental Cats

A Chocolate Oriental Spotted Tabby. These cats should look exactly the same as a Siamese but are accepted in different colors.

The various Siamese and Oriental breeds are without a doubt the extroverts of the pedigree cats. There is nothing average about a Siamese or Oriental; everything is over the top and larger than life. The Siamese is possibly the best known of all pedigree cats, and is certainly one of the oldest breeds. Its trademark is the pale body with darker markings on the face, ears, legs, and tail. The Siamese eyes are almond-shaped, slightly slanted, and a very vivid blue. In the Siamese of former times, crossed eyes was a common fault; in fact so common that it was considered to be a feature of the breed. These days, crosseyed Siamese are very seldom seen, as breeders have worked hard to remove this undesirable trait, and any crosseyed Siamese would be very heavily penalized at shows indeed.

The Siamese body is very long and slender—a long cat with tall, fine legs, and a long, whip-like tail. Again, in early Siamese one common feature was a kinked tail, but this is much less common these days. The coat is very short and sleek. The face is long, with a pointed muzzle and a profile without any break.

The Oriental breeds are of exactly the same conformation as the Siamese, only of other colors, and without the points.

Apart from their unusual, striking looks, the Siamese and Oriental cats are famous for their temperament. These are noisy cats, cats that talk back both to their owner and other cats, loudly demanding attention. Siamese and Orientals are very energetic and easily become bored if not stimulated enough. They do not like being on their own, and are at their happiest when in the company of like-minded cats. Very intelligent cats, these breeds will do almost anything to keep themselves amused, and they often work out tasks such as how to open closed doors. They adore human companionship and will happily snooze on their favorite person's lap when they are not engaged in a lively game. With their short coats, they often feel the cold more than other breeds, and a favorite resting place is in front of the radiator or fire.

Being such extrovert cats, Siamese and Orientals often find it difficult to get on with cats of very different temperament, such as the placid Persians. They do, however, often greatly enjoy the companionship of dogs.

The Siamese and Orientals require very little grooming. Brushing or combing is unnecessary; it is a better idea to polish the coat with a cloth now and then. There are some semi-longhairs within these breeds which will require a bit more grooming, but even this is minimal and usually confined to the tail, chest, and tummy areas.

Above: A group of Seal Point Siamese. The perfect Siamese cat is well-balanced with its head carried on a long svelte body. Its legs and feet, are long and fine and the tail in proportion. The head and profile are wedge-shapedand the eyes should be a brilliant blue.

Siamese

(AACE, ACA, ACFA, CFA, CFF, TICA, GCCF, CA)

The Siamese cat originates from Thailand, then known as Siam, sometime during the eighteenth century. The striking coloring of the Siamese, with its pale body and darker "points" (face, ears, legs, and tail) and bright blue eyes is not something that was created through deliberate breeding by man; it came about as a genetic mutation. The body becomes darker with age, especially within the darker colored varieties such as the SealPoint, but there is always an obvious difference between the points and the body color.

The slender and graceful Siamese has absolutely no tendency toward cobbiness. Everything about it is sleek, from the long, wedge-shaped head and pointed ears to its whippy, expressive tail. The coat is very short and smooth, much more so than in most shorthaired breeds.

The original Siamese was Seal Point; a creamy beige body (which gets darker with age) and dark seal brown points. These days, there are no fewer than 32 different color varieties in existence within the Siamese breed. Which colors that are recognized as true Siamese colorings, however, does vary between the different cat registration bodies. Several

Left: Blue Point Siamese. Although many people think of the typical Siamese cat as being Seal Point, the action of a gene mutation "dilutes" the seal colored points to a beautiful lavender blue.

consider a Siamese to be a pure Siamese only if it is either Seal Point, Blue Point, Chocolate Point, or Lilac Point—the four oldest colors.

The Siamese is an extrovert, a very vocal, energetic, playful, and highly intelligent cat. Life with a Siamese in the house is never dull, and a single Siamese is not happy unless the owner spends a lot of time with it, or provides a companion of the same or a similar breed.

Right: The paler colored Blue Point is a popular color variation in Great Britain.

Left: A Red Point Siamese.

Below Left: Known in the US as Lynx Point, the Tabby point Siamese is available in a wide variety of colors.

Balinese

(AACE, ACA, ACFA, CFA, CFF, TICA, GCCF, CA)

The Balinese is the semi-longhair version of the Siamese. Longhaired kittens were occasionally born within purebred Siamese litters during the 1940s, the result of a genetic mutation. These longhaired Siamese were kept for further breeding, and so the Balinese breed was born.

The Balinese is identical in looks to the Siamese with the single exception of the coat. Although the Balinese is semi-longhair it shows very little long coat; on the body it lays flat and in some Balinese the only noticeably longer fur is to be found on the tail. Others show a ruff of longer fur on the chest, particularly during colder weather. The Balinese body is slender and elegant, with long legs and a long tail. The head is long and wedge-shaped, the ears large.

The Balinese is seen in the same colors as the Siamese and, similarly, certain registries only accept the four original colors—Seal Point, Blue Point, Chocolate Point, and Lilac Point—to be true Balinese colors, although as many as 32 different colors do exist.

The Balinese is a demanding cat, always after attention and interaction from either its owner or likeminded cats. A highly energetic, curious, and intelligent cat, the Balinese is not happy left on its own.

Colorpoint Shorthair
(CFA)

The Colorpoint Shorthair is a Siamese cat of colors other than Seal Point, Blue Point, Chocolate Point or Lilac Point, the four original colors found in the Siamese breed. Most cat registries consider all 32 color variations to be purebred Siamese, but the CFA chose to recognize the newer colors as Colorpoint Shorthair. Thus, the Colorpoint Shorthair is identical in looks to the Siamese, with the same slender body and long face with tall ears. Typical colors include Flame Point, Cream Point, and also Lynx Points, which have tabby points.

Like all other Siamese, the Colorpoint Shorthair is a vocal and outgoing cat which demands a lot of attention.

Above: Some colors and patterns of Siamese are known as Colorpoint Shorthairs in the US. The Lynx Point (or Tabby Point) is one of these.

Above: The Javanese is an elegant cat with a fuller coat than its cousin, the Siamese.

Javanese

(CFA, CA)

Just as the Balinese is the semi-longhair version of the Siamese, the Javanese is the semi-longhair version of the Colorpoint Shorthair, i.e. a Balinese in colors not recognized as Balinese by the CFA or CA.

The Javanese has the slim, graceful body of the type, with long, thin legs and a long tail which should show a fine plume. The face is long and shows no break when viewed in profile, and the ears are large. On the body, the fur of the Javanese lies flat, but there may be a fuller neck ruff.

The Javanese is accepted in the same color variations as the Colorpoint Shorthair, with FlamePoints and LynxPoints being particularly popular.

The Javanese has an identical temperament to the Balinese; a real extrovert of a cat which craves companionship, attention, and playful games, and which makes its wishes clearly heard in a very loud voice indeed.

Right: This Blue Spotted Javanese has the fuller neck ruff that is a common trait of the breed.

Right: The White Oriental Shorthair is commonly known as the Foreign White.

Left: Long and elegant, the Oriental White is similar in looks to the Siamese but is bred for different colors.

Above: Ebony Silver Mackerel Tabby Oriental Shorthair. Tabby is a particularly popular color for this elegant breed which closely resembles the Siamese in all other respects.

Oriental Shorthair
(AACE, ACA, ACFA, CFA, CFF, TICA, GCCF, CA)

The Siamese is one of the ancestors of the Oriental Shorthair, along with ordinary non-pedigree shorthair cats. Accidental matings between Siamese and non-pedigrees produced kittens that were very much Siamese in body, but of other, non-pointed colors, and interested breeders decided to create a new breed from these striking cats.

The Oriental Shorthair has a body identical to that of the Siamese: medium-sized and very slender with long legs, a long, thin tail, a long face, and large ears. The fur is very short, sleek, and glossy. Many different colors can be seen in the breed, with selfs such as Black, White (known as the Foreign White), and Brown (known as the Havana) being particularly popular, as well as Tabbies.

The Oriental Shorthair is a cat with a lot of energy, a curious, playful, and intelligent breed which needs companionship to keep happy. Like the Siamese, it is a vocal breed.

Oriental Longhair, aka Angora

(AACE, ACA, TICA; registered as Angora with the GCCF)

The Oriental Longhair is a comparatively new breed of cat, developed in the 1990s. In the US, the breed was deliberately created as a semi-long-hair alternative to the Oriental Shorthair. The breed does exist in the UK, but is known as the Angora (a different breed from the Turkish Angora). The breed was created in the 1970s when crosses between Abyssinians and Siamese started to produce longhair kittens.

The Oriental Longhair is identical in looks to the Oriental Shorthair, showing the same long and elegant body with the long legs and wedge-shaped face. The one difference is in coat length; the Oriental Longhair has a plumed tail and a small ruff on the chest, but on the rest of the body the coat tends to lie flat. The same colors exist as in the Oriental Shorthair, with selfs being very popular.

The Oriental Longhair is a lively and curious cat which demands attention.

Above: The Oriental Longhair, or Angora as it is known in Great Britain. Colors are the same as in the Oriental Shorthair; accepted colors and patterns vary with the different registries.

Rex-coated Breeds

The very first cat with a curly, rex coat ever to appear was a Cornish Rex known as Kallibunker, born in Cornwall in England in 1950. Since then, many other rex breeds of cat has been discovered worldwide. What these breeds all have in common is that they have an unusual-looking curly or waved coat, and kittens are often more or less bald for several months before this coat starts to appear. However, the genes responsible for these various natural mutations are all different ones, and so it follows that if mating two rex cats of different breeds together, the resulting kittens will not be rex-coated but instead show an entirely normal, straight coat.

The looks of the various rex breeds also vary a lot. Some are long and slender with large ears, such as the Devon Rex, others are much cobbier with a short face, like the Selkirk Rex. Yet others are somewhere in between, like the American Wirehair, which is an altogether natural-looking cat with an average body, the only difference from the American Shorthair being its wavy coat. It is therefore impossible to generalize about what sort of temperament these different cats exhibit, as it will vary so much between the breeds. What they all have in common is that they require very little grooming. Shortcoated rex cats need no combing at all, just the occasional grooming session with a soft-bristled brush. The long-haired rex breeds will need more extensive brushing and also combing, but these breeds do not tend to be as prone to coat matting and tangling as straight-coated longhair breeds. Therefore, rex cats are generally speaking very "low maintenance" cats.

Of the different breeds, many have not yet expnded beyond their native countries, and it is only the two original breeds, the Cornish Rex and the Devon Rex, which have a worldwide popularity.

Right The coat of the Cornish Rex should be short and plushy, silken in texture, without guard hairs and must wave, curl, or ripple particularly on the back and tail.

Right: American Wirehair kitten.

American Wirehair
(ACA, ACFA, CFA, TICA)

The first American Wirehair kitten was born in 1961, a mutated kitten born to ordinary non-pedigree cats in New York.

The American Wirehair has a body which is medium in all ways; the body of the average moggy. The breed is medium or large, heavy, and well-muscled. The coat of the American Wirehair is unlike most other rex coats seen in cats. It is heavily waved as opposed to curly, and is also very dense. Whereas most rex cats have a very soft coat, the American Wirehair should feel harsh to the touch.

The American Wirehair is accepted in virtually all colors, only the pointed Siamese pattern and Chocolate or Lilac cats are considered unacceptable.

The American Wirehair is a quiet and undemanding breed of cat, friendly and loyal toward its owner but somewhat reserved in the company of strangers.

Cornish Rex
(AACE, ACA, ACFA, CFA, CFF, TICA, GCCF, CA)
This is the oldest known breed of rex-coated cat, having first appeared as a spontaneous mutation in Cornwall, England, in 1950.

The Cornish Rex is slender yet not as slim as the Siamese, a cat of medium size, with a fairly average head shape and tall ears. The body feels heavier than it looks and must be muscular. The coat of the Cornish Rex is soft to the touch and should be curled all over the body. Kittens and younger cats may show varying degrees of baldness. All colors and markings are accepted in the breed.

The Cornish Rex is a very friendly and outgoing breed of cat with a high level of curiosity. They love athletic games such as chasing after balls or climbing and jumping.

Above: Tabby Cornish Rex.

Right: Red Cornish Rex.

Left: Red Cornish Rex.

Above: Black Smoke Devon Rex.

Devon Rex
(AACE, ACA, ACFA, CFA, CFF, GCCF, CA)

In 1960, ten years after the first Cornish Rex had been discovered, the first Devon Rex appeared in neighboring Devon. It was originally believed that the two rex breeds were caused by the same mutated gene, as the coats were similar in looks, but when Cornish and Devon Rexes were mated together only kittens with normal coats were produced, thus proving that the Devon Rex was caused by a different gene from that of the Cornish Rex.

The Devon Rex is more exaggerated in looks that the Cornish Rex, and is often described as being pixie-like in appearance. The head is short and wide, with ears that are oversized and prominent. The Devon Rex is medium in size and very muscular, with a body that is slender but not slim. The coat is very soft and must be curled or waved all over the body. Kittens and young adults may be almost completely bald for long periods of time, but the coat does grow out in most cases once the cat is more mature. Any color, pattern or markings can be found in the Devon Rex.

The Devon Rex shows a great zest for life, an outgoing and extremely friendly cat that wants to be included in whatever is going on.

Above: Black Smoke Devon Rex.

Left: These Devon Rex kittens show the breed's variety of colors and markings.

Right: **To keep the Devon Rex's coat in perfect condition like the cat shown, the cat must have a good well-balanced diet. Despite the curls grooming is easy and a soft brush will remove any dead hair that might make the coat less lustrous.**

LaPerm

Above: Brown Torbie LaPerm.

(ACFA)

The first LaPerm kitten was born to non-pedigree parents in Dallas in the early 1980s. Controlled breeding was not carried out for several years, yet more kittens of this rex-coated breed started to appear naturally, and eventually a breeding program was started.

The LaPerm is an unusual rex breed in that, along with the Selkirk Rex, it can be either shorthaired or longhaired. The coat is very soft and shows tight curls. The body of the LaPerm is somewhat Foreign in type, but with no exaggerations. Any color is acceptable.

The LaPerm is a friendly and docile cat which loves the company of people and other cats.

Above: Black Selkirk Rex.

Selkirk Rex

(ACFA, ACA, CFA, TICA)

The Selkirk Rex was discovered in 1987, when a non-pedigree queen in a cat shelter in Wyoming gave birth to a curly-coated kitten. This kitten was acquired by an interested Persian breeder who crossed it with her Persian cats. The result is the largest of the rex-coated breeds, being medium to large in size with a rounded body and head. Due to its Persian ancestry, the head is broad with a fairly short nose. The curling of the coat is loose, the coat is dense and stands out from the cat's body, and it can be either short or long. The Selkirk Rex is accepted in any color or markings.

The Selkirk Rex is friendly, playful, and generally a laid-back cat with a docile temperament.

Above: Silver Chocolate Lynx Point Selkirk Rex.

Left: Brown Tabby Selkirk Rex.

Other Breeds

The breeds listed here are those that for one reason or another do not quite fit under any of the other breed headings. These breeds are mainly cats that are different in any sort of way, such as the Sphynx with no fur, the Japanese Bobtail with its short and curled tail, the Munchkin with its stumpy legs, and the Scottish Fold with its folded-down ears. None of these breeds is accepted by the UK's Governing Council of the Cat Fancy, and most would be or have been rejected by it.

Needless to say, it is impossible to generalize about the looks, care, and general behavior of such a diversity of breeds.

Far Right: The cross-bred Pixiebob is a courageous and loyal cat claimed by its admirers to guard their owners and their homes from harm, yet still a loving, family-oriented animal.

Right: The seemingly hairless Sphynx Cat is whiskerless but is actually covered with very fine, down-like fur. Its skin needs to be kept in good condition and out of the sunshine.

Above: American Bobtail.

American Bobtail
(ACFA, TICA)

This short-tailed breed breed came about as a spontaneous genetic mutation; the first Bobtail kitten was born to ordinary farm cats in Arizona. The breed was recognized by TICA in 1989.

The American Bobtail is a natural-looking cat of medium size without any exaggerations in body or build. It is muscular but neither lean nor cobby. The head is of average length and shape, but the brow is heavier than in most breeds, which gives the cat a wild look. The coat can be either short or semi-long, and in the longhair Bobtail it should look shaggy and must be water-repellent. The tail is short but not non-existent, and this should stand erect. The American Bobtail is accepted in all colors and markings.

The American Bobtail is a cat that shows loyalty and affection toward its owner, but which greets strangers with suspicion.

Left: American Curl.

American Curl

(AACE, ACA, ACFA, CFA, CFF, TICA)

The American Curl originates from California, where the first curly-eared kitten was born in 1981. The exact origins are unknown, as the very first American Curl was found as a stray.

The American Curl is an elegant cat of medium size; slender but not lean. The head is fairly long. The coat can be either short or semi-long. The most important feature of this breed is its ears, which curl backwards. The ears are measured according to how heavy a curl they show: a first degree curl is a light curl at the very tip of the ears, a second degree curl curls backwards at between 45 and 90 degrees, and the show-quality third degree curl shows a 90–180-degree curl, with the tips pointing toward the centre of the base of the skull, but without touching the back of the head. The breed is accepted in all colors.

This is a playful breed which loves to chase balls and play similar games. It is an intelligent and very friendly cat.

Above: Cymric.

Cymric

(AACE, ACA, ACFA, TICA, CA)

The Cymric is the longhaired version of the Manx cat. Unlike the Manx, this breed was developed (in the 1960s) in the US and not in the UK. The Manx is part of the British Shorthair breed group in the UK under GCCF rules, so cannot be accepted as a longhair. However, it is believed that, originally, Manx cats were seen as both shorthairs and longhairs.

A cat of medium size, the Cymric is hardy and natural-looking. The back is short and the hind legs longer than the front legs, giving the Cymric a rabbit-like gait. There is no tail at all in show-quality specimens. The head is round with full cheeks, but not quite as broad as that of the Manx. The coat is soft and very dense, slightly fuller on the chest than on the rest of the body. All colors except for the pointed Himalayan pattern are accepted in the breed.

The Cymric is a friendly cat with an easygoing nature, neither overly energetic nor lazy.

Japanese Bobtail
(AACE, ACA, ACFA, CFA, CFF, TICA, CA)

The Japanese Bobtail is believed to be a naturally occurring ancient breed, which was first imported to the US from Japan in 1968. The breed is not seen in the UK.

It is a slender yet muscular cat of medium size, with a face that is fairly long and shows high cheekbones. The Japanese Bobtail can be either shorthaired or semi-longhaired. The tail is very important. It should look similar to a rabbit's tail: no more than 3 in long, and it is usually curved or angled.

The Japanese Bobtail is popularly seen as either White, Black, Red, Black and White, Red and White, Mi-ke (Tri-color), or Tortoiseshell. Other colors do occur at times, and most are accepted, with a few exceptions.

The Bobtail is intelligent, playful, and outgoing, and the breed matures quickly.

Above: Black and White Japanese Bobtail.

Above: Munchkin.

Munchkin
(ACFA, TICA)

The Munchkin is named after the little people in *The Wizard of Oz*, and is a breed which can be likened to a dwarf. The Munchkin appeared as a spontaneous mutation during the 1980s in Rayville, Louisiana.

Essentially, the Munchkin looks like any moggy or non-pedigree cat, with an average body and head. The very obvious exception is the legs, which are very short, similar to the legs of a Dachshund. The legs are roughly half the length of other cats' legs, and the elbows are held high and close to the body. Obviously, the Munchkin walks in an entirely different way from other cats, and also finds it more difficult to jump and climb. Any color is accepted.

The Munchkin has deliberately been bred to retain kitten-like characteristics and behavior throughout its life, and it is a friendly and playful breed.

Pixiebob

(ACA, TICA)

The Pixiebob came about as a cross between domestic cats and the bob-cat, a small wild cat that resembles a lynx. Such matings had taken place for several years, but it was not until the 1970s that breeders started a controlled breeding program to further develop this cat, which came to be named the Pixiebob.

Although it still shows many characteristics of a wild cat, the Pixiebob is bred to be a reliable and friendly pet cat. It is medium to large in size, with a muscular and rangy-looking body. The head has heavy brows, deepset eyes, and a long but broad muzzle, all going to create the impression of a wild-looking cat. The Pixiebob comes in both shorthair and longhair. The coat in the longhair is softer than in the shorthair, without a neck ruff, and it is water-resistant. The tail is short, either kinked or knotted, and the length equals the distance from the hip bone to the base of the tail. The color is always Brown Spotted Tabby.

The Pixiebob is a cat of loyalty and courage, more like a dog than a cat in behavior; it is even said to guard its owner's house from intruders—yet must be perfectly reliable within the family.

Above: Brown Patched Tabby and White Longhair Scottish Fold. The longhaired cat is accepted by some registries as the Highland Fold.

Scottish Fold

(AACE, ACA, ACFA, CFA, CFF, TICA)

The first Scottish Fold originated in Scotland, but is far more widely spread in the US as the GCCF decided to deregister the breed. The first Scottish Fold kitten to be born was a white female, on Tayside in 1961. The breed has been extensively outcrossed both to British and American Shorthairs.

The Scottish Fold is a medium-sized cat, with a rounded and cobby body, together with a rounded head not dissimilar to that of early Persians. The all-important ears can be either straight, show a single fold (with the tips of the ears bending forward about halfway up the ear), a double fold, or a triple fold, where the ears are closely folded down.

The coat can be either short or semi-long; the AACE and ACFA recognize the longhaired variety as the Highland Fold. The CFF accepts all colors and patterns of the Scottish Folds, but other registries do not allow for the pointed Himalayan pattern.

The Scottish Fold is a friendly and loving cat, fairly docile yet playful.

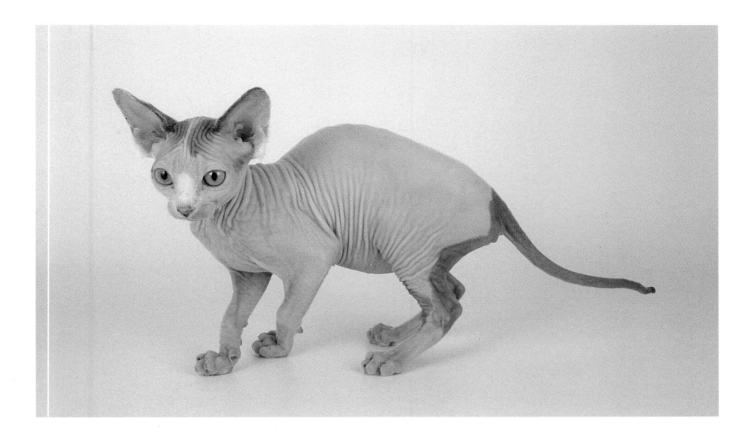

Sphynx

(AACE, ACA, ACFA, CFA, TICA)

The hairless cat is a phenomenon which has occurred from time to time during history. When a hairless kitten was born in Canada interested breeders decided to develop the gene for hairlessness further, and the Sphynx was recognized as an actual breed of cat in 1966.

The Sphynx is a cat very much like a Siamese or Oriental in shape. It is medium in size with a long and slender body, long, slim legs, a thin tail, a long triangular face and large ears. At a first glance, the Sphynx appears to be entirely hairless, but on closer inspection it can be seen that the cat is indeed covered by very fine, down-like fur. The skin is normally wrinkled and this is sought after in show specimens, as is the lack of whiskers. Any color or pattern is accepted, but the lack of real fur naturally means it can be quite difficult to tell which color the Sphynx is.

The Sphynx is energetic and curious, a highly intelligent and playful cat which craves company. Its unprotected skin needs to be kept in good condition, and Sphynx cats should ideally not be allowed outside.

Above: Often called "hairless," the Sphynx is in fact covered by a soft coat described as "peach-like."

Reference

Cat Magazines

UK

Your Cat: This is Britain's best selling cat magazine. Published every month it has excellent articles on different breeds, tips on caring for your cat, and understanding feline behavior. It also has great photography.

Cat World: Another good magazine. It is worth looking at their website at www.catworld.co.uk where you can sample what the magazine has to offer.

USA

Cats: A monthly magazine for "people who love cats," like *Your Cat* in the UK it is packed with interesting and fun information, expert help, and great photos. They also have a website, at www.catsmag.com.

Cat Fancy: For further information you can email catfancy@fancypubs.com.

Cats and Kittens: Their website at www.catsandkittens.com allows you to order a free sample of the magazine.

Persian News: A specialist magazine for the Persian owner. Their website is at www.persiannews.hypermart.net

A Red Burmese. Cats of this breed are extremely playful and energetic and will seem to eat twice as much as any other breed due to their exertions!

Cat Registering Organizations

UK

The Governing Council of the Cat Fancy (GCCF)
4-6, Penel Orlieu, Bridgwater, Somerset, TA6 3PG (UK)
TELEPHONE: (0)1278 427 575
Email: GCCF_CATS@compuserve.com

The Cat Association of Britain (CA)
Member of FIFe
General enquiries to:
Mr C Clarke
Mill House, Letcombe Regis, Wantage, Oxon OX12 9JD, UK
TELEPHONE: (0)1235 766543

USA
American Cat Association (ACA)
8101 Katherine
Panorama City, CA 01402

American Cat Fanciers Association (ACFA)
P.O. Box 203
Manasquan, NJ 08738

Cat Fanciers Association, Inc. (CFA)
P.O. Box 1005
Manasquan, NJ
08736-0805
http://www.cfainc.org/cfa/

Cat Fanciers Federation (CFF)
9509 Montgomery Rd.
Cincinnati, OH 45242

The International Cat Association (TICA)
P.O. Box 2684
Harlingen, TX 78551
www.alaka.net/~denalimc/tica.html

Cat Internet Sites

There are literally hundreds of web sites dedicated to cats—breeds, care, shows, and any other information that you could possibly want. If you have ever "surfed" though you will know that the only difficulty can be in locating the right pages! However, it can be fun looking and you might come across some interesting sites along the way. These are a few of the best.

www.thepetchannel.com/
www.petstation.com
www.acmepet.com
www.vetinfo.com
www.fanciers.com
http://catlovers.com/
http://loki.stockton.edu/~stk10693/home.html
www.voicenet.com/~billpiel/cat/
http://excite.netscape.com/directory/kids_and_family/pets/cats/

http://www.avma.org/care4pets/ppetcat.htm
http://www.io.com/~tittle/cat-faqs/
http://www.thegalleries.com/petlover/index-cats.html
http://members.aol.com/catsbuzz/

Books About Cats

Beylani, C.; *A Literary Companion to Cats*; Sinclair Stevenson.

Caufield, J., and others; *Chicken Soup for the Pet Lover's Soul*; Random House.

Cooper, P. and Noble, P.; *277 Secrets Your Cat Wants You to Know*; 10 Speed Press.

Edney, A.; *Complete Cat Care Manual*; Dorling Kinderesley.

Fogle, Dr. B.; *Natural Cat Care*; Dorling Kindersley.

Giant Book of the Cat; Chartwell.

Jalik, C. and Regnis, R.; *The Complete Idiot's Guide to Living with a Cat*; Alpha Books.

Maggitti, P.; *The Cat*; Tiger Books.

Milani, M., DVM; *Catsmart*; Contemporary Books.

Morris, D.; *Catwatching*; Cape.

Shojai, A.; *Kitten Care and Training*; Howell Book House.

Shreck, M.; *Kittens; A Portrait of the Animal World*; Todtri.

Spadafori, G. and Pion, P., DVM, DACVIM; *Cats For Dummies*; IDG Books.

Tabor, R.; *Understanding Cats*; David & Charles.

Taylor, D.; *The Ultimate Cat Book*; Dorling Kindersley.

The American Animal Hospital Association; *Encyclopedia of Cat Health and Care*; Quill.

The Complete Cat Owner's Manual; HarperCollins.

The Reader's Digest *Illustrated Book of Cats*; Reader's Digest.